Jazmin Kazi-Haque

TeXt

Building skills in English

BOOK 1

Annabel Charles • Richard Durant • David Grant
Esther Menon • Beverly Turner

Consultant: Cindy Torn

D1638320

www.heinemann.co.uk

✓ Free online support
✓ Useful weblinks
✓ 24 hour online ordering

01865 888118

Contents

Contents

1 A life's story

Objectives

In this unit you will:

Reading
- use skimming and scanning to find information in a text
- make notes when gathering ideas from a text
- identify and understand the main ideas in a text
- distinguish between fact and opinion.

Composition
- organise texts to make their meaning clear
- use punctuation accurately in clauses and sentences
- use well structured paragraphs to make your ideas clear
- use a range of linking words and phrases to lead through a text.

Conventions
- understand the use of tense in standard English and use it in your writing.

Language
- understand and use the terms noun, verb and adverb.

By the end of this unit you will:
- get information from sources and make notes (Reading: Reading for meaning)
- write a biography (Writing: Composition and conventions).

Cross-curricular links
- **History**
  Using evidence
- **Citizenship**
  Advocacy and representation; Critical thinking and enquiry

1 Biography and autobiography

An autobiography is the story of someone's life written by that person. A biography is the story of someone's life written by someone else. When we read autobiographies and biographies we learn about a person's life. We may be inspired by their achievements, or we may just learn more about their everyday life.

Activity 1

Look at the front covers of these biographies and autobiographies.

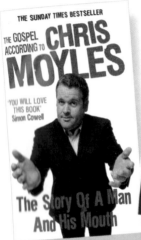

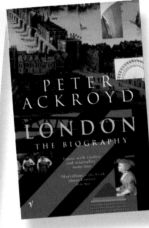

1   Using a table like the one below, decide which are autobiographies and which are biographies. Make sure you can justify your choices.

	Biography (✓)	Autobiography (✓)	What are your reasons?
1			
2			

2   Which one does not fit either category?

Activity 2

A blurb tells people about a book's contents to encourage them to buy it.

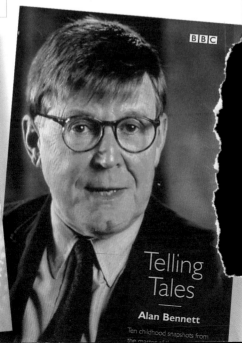

1   Read the blurbs from the two autobiographies shown here and look at their front covers on page 6.
    a   What kind of audience do you think the blurb is written for and why?
    b   Who might the front cover appeal to?
    c   What kind of readers might be interested in the topics, such as fashion or family life, that are mentioned in these blurbs?
    d   Which words and phrases in each blurb have been written to appeal to that audience?

Blurb A

Her story is a Cinderella Fairytale of an ordinary Liverpudlian school girl who was transformed into a style icon and cover girl, sought after by fashion and lifestyle magazines the world over.

Welcome to my World is Coleen's chance to reflect on this amazing journey and share her love of fashion with her fans. From puffa jackets to Prada bags, Coleen reveals the secrets behind her famous wardrobe, her style, her guide to shopping, her do's and don'ts, her beauty regimes and her body workouts. It's also the story of a young girl who has managed to keep true to her working-class roots whilst being catapulted into a world beyond her wildest dreams.'

– From *Welcome to My World*
by Coleen McLoughlin

Blurb B

Alan Bennett recalls his childhood in a sequence of tales that are funny, touching and told in his unique style. Hampered as he sees it by a family that never manages to be quite like other families, he recounts his early years in Leeds – a place where early in life one learned the quite useful lesson that 'life is generally something that happens elsewhere'. Hiking every Sunday, trips into town and teas in cafes, it's an ordinary childhood – his father a butcher, his mother a reader of women's magazines who dreams of coffee mornings, cocktail parties and life 'down south'.

Here Alan Bennett relives family crises, early pieties and the lost tradition of musical evenings around the piano, with the wry observation and ironic understatement that has earned him a place in the forefront of contemporary writing.

– From *Telling Tales*
by Alan Bennett

2   Some public figures have a 'ghost writer', a professional writer who either improves their autobiography or writes the vast majority of it for them. Which of the texts above do you think is more likely to have had a ghost writer and why?

Sharpen your skills Nouns and verbs

Nouns tell us the name of something or someone.
Nouns usually have *a*, *an* or *the* in front of them.
A verb tells us what a person or thing does.

Look again at Blurb A.
1   Can you identify the nouns in the last sentence? How many are there?
2   How many proper nouns are there in the second sentence?
3   Can you identify the verbs in the first two sentences?

2 Reading and researching

You are learning:
- to find the information you need.

Skimming and scanning are important reading skills. **Skimming** helps you read quickly to get the overall gist of a text to decide whether it contains the information you need.

Scanning is a way of looking for specific information in a text. You do not need to read every word. You can use headings and titles to help you locate your information. This is a reading skill you use when you look words up in a dictionary, or search for telephone numbers in a directory.

Activity 1

1 Read the research topics in the table below. Skim page 9, which is taken from the poet Benjamin Zephaniah's personal website. Decide how useful the page would be if you were researching the topics in the table below. Try to do this in two minutes.

 2 minutes

Research topic	Useful? Yes (✓) No (✗)
a Facts about Zephaniah's professional achievements	
b Interviews with Zephaniah	
c Information about the type of poetry Zephaniah writes and performs	
d Blurbs from Zephaniah's novels for teenagers	
e Information about Zephaniah's childhood	
f Pictures and details of his friends and contacts	

A Poet Called Benjamin Zephaniah

http://www.benjaminzephaniah.com/truth.html

Full Name: Benjamin Obadiah Iqbal Zephaniah
Place of Birth: Birmingham/England
Occupation: Poet/Writer
Hobbies: Martial arts, Numismatics
Poetry: *Pen Rhythm*. London, Page One, 1980
The Dread Affair. London, Arena, 1985; *Inna Liverpool*. Liverpool, Africa Arts Collective, 1988; *City Psalms*. Newcastle, Bloodaxe, 1992; *Talking Turkeys*. London, Puffin/Penguin, 1994 (children's); *Out of the Night*. Gloucester, New Clarion Press. 1994 (Co-editor – *Writings from Death Row*); *Funky Chickens*. London, Puffin/Penguin, 1996 (children's); *Propa Propaganda*. Newcastle, Bloodaxe, 1996; *School's Out*. Edinburgh, AK Press, 1997 (big children); *The Bloomsbury Book of Love Poems*. London, Bloomsbury, 1999 (editor); *Wicked World*. London, Puffin/Penguin, 2000 (children's); *The Little Book of Vegan Poems*. Edinburgh, AK Press, 2001; *Too Black, Too Strong*. Newcastle, Bloodaxe, 2001; *We are Britain*. Francis Lincoln, 2002
Novels: *Gangsta Rap*, Bloomsbury, 2004; *Face*. London, Bloomsbury, 1999 (teenagers); *Refugee Boy*. London, Bloomsbury, 2001 (teenagers)
Prose: *Rasta Time in Palestine*. Liverpool, Shakti, 1990
Records: *Dub Ranting – Radical Wallpaper*, 1982; *Rasta LP – Upright*, 1983; *Big Boys Don't Make Girls Cry* – Upright 1984; *Free South Africa* – Upright, 1986; *Us An Dem* LP – Mango, 1990; *Crisis* – Workers Playtime, 1992; *Back to Roots* LP – Acid Jazz, 1995; *Belly of De Beast* LP – Ariwa, 1996; *Dancing Tribes* (with Back to Base). (Single) MP Records, 1999; *Illegal* (with Swayzak). (Single) Medicine Label, 2000
Spoken Word Cassettes: *Radical Rapping*. Benjamin Zephaniah Associates, 1989; *Overstanding*. Benjamin Zephaniah Associates, 1992; *Adult Fun for Kids*. Benjamin Zephaniah Associates, 1994 (big children); *Reggae Head*. 57 Productions, 1997; *Funky Turkeys*. Audio Book and Music Company, 1997 (children's); *Wicked World*. Penguin, 2000 (children's)
Plays:
Stage *Listen to Your Parents* (adapted from radio play); *Playing the Right Tune*, 1985; *Job Rocking*, 1987; *Delirium*, 1987 (dance); *Streetwise*, 1990; *Mickey Tekka*, 1991 (children's)
Radio *Face* – Radio Four (adapted from novel); *Hurricane Dub* – BBC, 1989; *Our Teacher's Gone Crazy* – BBC, 1990; *Listen to Your Parents* – BBC Radio, 2000
Television *Dread Poets Society* – BBC, 1991

Oral Poetry

I have been called a dub poet, an oral poet, a performance poet, a pop poet, a pub poet, a rap poet, a Rasta poet, a reggae poet and even a black poet, the list goes on. In all honesty, none of those titles offend me, I am probably all of these persons but if I had to choose one I would start with oral poet. I say this because as I write my poetry, I can hear the sound of it,

Dub Poetry

If you can see poetry as a tree with many branches and oral poetry as one of those branches, then a leaf on that branch could be Dub poetry. Dub poetry has its roots in Jamaica and is closely linked to Reggae music. Dub poetry is political, no one made this rule, that's just the way it is and poets like myself, Linton Kwesi Johnson, Jean Breeze, Oku Onuora and Lillian Allen all worked in community groups which gave us our first audiences.

The oral poet's relationship with the audience is most important, she or he has to read the audience and be able to fully communicate and deliver the message. We oral poets do get published now but knowing that reading is a minority pastime, it would be fair to say that the publishing of books is way down on our list of priorities. We put poetry into music, into plays. On television, radio, we perform like crazy people, we put poems on postcards and in micro chips, in fact we do anything to change the dead, white and boring image of poetry.

2   Look again at page 9. Where on this web page would you click to find information on the following research topics? Use a table like the one below. Try to do this in two minutes.

 2 minutes

Research topic	What I would click on
Information on Zephaniah's novels for teenagers	Teenz
Examples of Zephaniah's poems	
People and personal contacts that are part of Zephaniah's life	
Examples and cuttings of media articles on the poet	

Activity 2

This picture summarises Zephaniah's opinions on Dub and Rap poetry. Scan Zephaniah's web page to find the information you need to complete the picture.

The following questions will help you select your information.

1   What does Zephaniah say is the leaf attached to the branch of oral poetry?

2   Which country is the root of dub poetry?

3   Who are the other dub poets that first performed to audiences with Zephaniah?

4   Where would you be able to find their dub poetry?

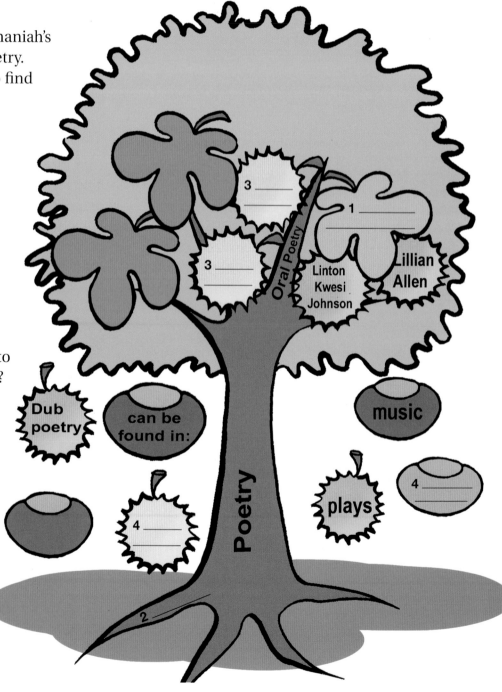

Assess your progress

Look at the skills you have been practising on pages 8 to 10. How well are you doing? Pick the traffic light that shows how confident you feel in each area.

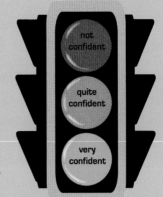

- I understand the difference between skimming and scanning.
- I can use skimming skills to decide whether a text might be relevant for what I need.
- I can use scanning skills to find and select specific information.
- I can identify examples in the text that support my opinions.

Sharpen your skills · Capital letters and full stops

Read the biographical details below on the dub poet Linton Kwesi Johnson. Use what you have learnt about full stops and capital letters to correct the errors in the passage.

Remember:

- Every sentence must begin with a capital letter.
- Proper nouns must begin with a capital letter.
- Use a full stop to end any sentence which is not a question or an exclamation.

Linton Kwesi Johnson was born on 24 august 1952 in jamaica. He came to london in 1963, went to Tulse Hill secondary school and later studied at goldsmiths' college, University of London

When he was still at school he joined the black panthers, which was an organization that started in America to support the rights of black people He helped to organize a poetry workshop within the movement and developed his work with a group of poets and drummers called rasta Love. He published three collections of poems before launching his own record label in 1981, during the 1980s he was involved in journalism.

linton kwesi johnson has been made an Associate Fellow of warwick University, an Honorary Fellow of wolverhampton polytechnic and received an award at the XIII Premo Internazionale Ultimo Novecento from the city of pisa for his contribution to poetry and popular music (1990). He has toured the world and his work has been translated into italian and german,. he is famous as the world's first dub poet

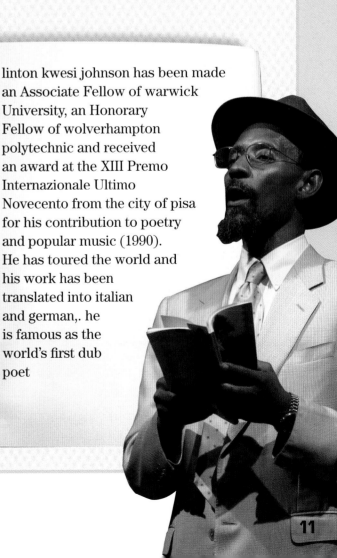

3 Note-making

You are learning:
- to identify and note down key points.

Making notes can help you make sense of a text. It can also improve your memory of what you have read. It helps you to write the key learning points in your own words, without copying out a text in full.

Activity 1

Thomas Edison was one of the world's greatest inventors. Amongst other things, he invented the phonograph (the first device for recording and replaying sound), the first commercially produced electric lightbulb, the typewriter and the motion picture camera.

1 Read the biographical information about the childhood of Thomas Edison.

Thomas Alva Edison

Some thought he 'wasn't quite right in the head'.

He was born in 1847 in Milan, Ohio, and even as a young boy, his curiosity was always getting him into trouble.

He always wanted to know 'why'. At age three he fell into a grain elevator and almost drowned in the grain because he wanted to see how the elevator worked. And at age four, his father found him squatting on some duck eggs in a cold barn to see if he could hatch the eggs instead of the mother duck.

He had very little formal education because his teachers thought his constant questions were a sign of stupidity. So when he was seven, his mother, who had been a teacher, took him out of school and taught him at home.

Some of the neighbours thought this strange child with the small body and unusually large head who asked so many questions must be 'addled', and even the local doctor feared he might have 'brain trouble' because of his very large head.

He loved to read and chemistry books were his favourite books, but he did more than just read them. He tried many of the experiments the books described to prove to himself that the facts in the books were really true.

When he was about ten, he set up a chemistry lab in the basement in his home, and during one of his experiments, he set the basement on fire and nearly blew himself up.

Then when he was twelve, in order to earn money to pay for the chemicals for his experiments, he went into business selling candy and newspapers to the local train and worked on his scientific experiments in his spare time.

He was forced to stop his experiments temporarily when a stick of phosphorous started a fire in the crude lab he had set up in the baggage car; the conductor threw him and his equipment off the train at the next stop.

It seemed he was always experimenting. Once he gave a friend a triple dose of **seidlitz powders**, hoping that enough gas would be generated to enable him to fly. This resulted in terrible agonies for his friend and a whipping for him.

At sixteen he was given the chance to learn how to be a telegraph operator, and he then became as fascinated by electricity as he had been with chemistry.

Explanations

seidlitz powders a mixture of chemicals that are very fizzy when mixed with water
key words words that summarise the information contained in the main topic

– From *Dare to Dream: 25 extraordinary lives* by Sandra McLeod Humphrey

2 Write down five **key words** that sum up Edison's childhood.

3 Now close this book and expand your key words by writing a paragraph of notes from memory.

4 Summarise what you have learnt about Edison's childhood.

Activity 2

The text about Thomas Edison is organised chronologically, which means that events are described in the order in which they occurred. Use a timeline like the one illustrated here to summarise key points in Edison's life and how they predicted his future genius.

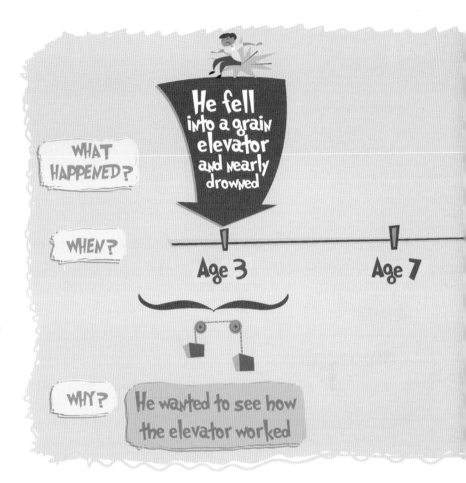

Sharpen your skills   Sequencing

The points below summarise key points about Thomas Edison's adult life. Put them into the correct order. Write down the word or words that helped you correctly place each section in the sequence.

1 In 1879 he showed his greatest invention, the first incandescent light that was practical for society to use. Other inventors had produced electric lighting in laboratories, but none produced lights that were long-lasting enough to be sold to consumers.

2 On the day he died, the American President asked everyone in America to turn off their electric lights for one hour, as a tribute to his genius.

4 A year later he introduced his first great invention, the phonograph, to the world.

3 In 1876 he moved to New Jersey, to a larger place where he could expand his work. He established his own research centre there.

5 By the age of 21 he had changed from an experimenter to inventor and worked full-time on his inventions.

4 Fact and opinion

You are learning:
- to distinguish between fact and opinion.

A fact is something that is true. An opinion is somebody's point of view.

Activity 1

1   Read these two texts about Shaun Ellis. Text A gives information about his life. Text B is a TV channel's introduction to a programme before it is broadcast.

Text A

Biography

Shaun Ellis is a man in wolf's clothing, living wild with them and talking their language… literally. For a raw meat-eating 'wild animal' used to roaming his environment by night and marking his territory wherever he pleases, Shaun Ellis comes across as a surprisingly civilised individual. Well-spoken, intelligent and passionate, it's only the excessively shaggy beard and straggly hair that gives him away as one of the leading members of a pack of wolves.

Three years ago, the 42-year-old decided the only way to really get to know his beloved wolves was to become one of them. He entered an enclosure at a wildlife park in North Devon, along with three abandoned new-born cubs, and became the alpha male of the group, raising the small family as his own. For the first 18 months, he was in the enclosure 24/7 and even now spends most of his time, and almost all of his evenings, huddled up alongside his wolf family.

He has learned to eat raw meat straight off the carcass of a dead animal, communicate with them by howling and is covered in scratches and wounds from his playful wrestles and fights with his 'brothers'.

But as unusual a lifestyle as this sounds, this is not some mid-life crisis, breakdown or attempt to turn his back on society. Shaun's adventure has been a long-standing scientific study into the lifestyle of his favourite animal and has so far produced some incredible results.

Eventually, he hopes to put his findings to good use and boost the campaign to reintroduce wild wolves to areas such as the Highlands, where they haven't been seen living free for hundreds of years.

He feels that working with animals and trying to understand how they live is what he was put on this planet to do and he has travelled the world to get closer to nature.

Text B

Wolf Man

Explore the crazy world of wolf-man and researcher Shaun Ellis, who has lived among wolves to research the way they live. In our unmissable documentary, *Wolf Man*, watch the extraordinary behaviour of this man, who has left his everyday life to live amongst beasts as he becomes leader of the pack, learns their ways and acts like them. An opportunity to have an amazing insight into his unique life and these fascinating animals!

2 Text A is a recount text and contains facts to inform the reader. In the table below are the features of a recount text. Find an example of each feature in Text A.

Feature of recount text	Example
Events written in time order (chronological order)	
Connectives related to time (e.g. later, twenty years on)	
Dialogue or reported speech to reveal information about the character	
Specific dates, times, people and places	
Answers to the questions when, where, who, what, why	

3 Text B contains writing to persuade. The writer of this text chooses words which he or she hopes will persuade people to watch the programme. Can you find phrases that show the writer's opinions?

4 Which of the two texts would be more useful and reliable if you were researching the life of Shaun Ellis? Give reasons for your answer.

Assess your progress

A key skill in reading and research is being able to use evidence from texts to 'back up' your views.

How confident were you in completing questions 2 and 3 above? Look again at the quotations you picked. Are they effective evidence for the questions you were asked? You might like to discuss your choices with a partner and compare your selections.

Choose the traffic light that shows how confident you feel in selecting evidence.

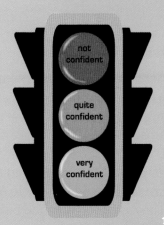

5 Gathering evidence

You are learning:
- to decide where you might find relevant information and to then select what you need.

Information is now available in far more ranges and formats than in the past: film, radio, TV, the Internet, ICT resources, books, newspapers and magazines. It is important to be able to know where to find what you need, select what is useful and then organise it.

Activity 1

You are going to complete a research task to understand more about autism. Use a diagram like the one here to summarise what you already **know** about autism, what you **think** you know about it, and what you want to **find out** about it.

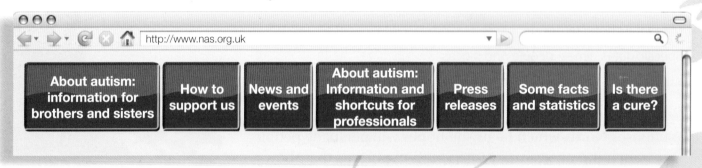

Activity 2

Below are links from the National Autistic Society website. Which of the linked pages would be most useful for finding out facts about autism? Give reasons for your choice.

http://www.nas.org.uk

| About autism: information for brothers and sisters | How to support us | News and events | About autism: Information and shortcuts for professionals | Press releases | Some facts and statistics | Is there a cure? |

Activity 3

The following extract describes the writer's experience with their brother, who is autistic. Read the extract, then create a diagram like the one in Activity 1, using the information you have read about autism.

Communication

Okay, let's start with number one, **difficulty with communication**. Some people with autism do not speak, or some people have difficulty speaking. For those that do not speak, they may use pictures, written words or even something called sign language (hand or arm movements) to tell people what they need or how they are feeling.

My brother sometimes takes my hand or shows me what he wants instead of speaking because he finds this easier to do. My brother can speak but sometimes it takes him a long time to say something back to me. If I say lots of words at once, he can become very confused, so I must remember to keep things simple and sometimes say things slowly.

My brother also has problems working out when someone is joking or teasing him. To help him understand jokes, I sometimes have to say that I was joking.

We understand how people are feeling by looking at their faces. My brother and people with autism find it very hard to understand faces. For example, my brother doesn't seem to know when I'm angry or upset.

Sometimes he copies or even laughs at me. He doesn't mean this to be horrible, he just doesn't know what to do when I am feeling like this. Sometimes he thinks I'm just pulling a funny face, which is why he laughs at me, but a lot of the time he doesn't realise that he should help me or leave me alone.

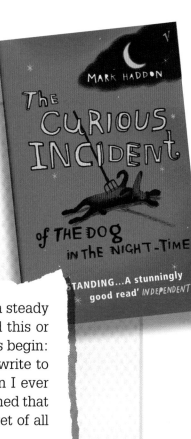

Sharpen your skills The past tense

Autobiographies and biographies are recount texts and are usually written in the past tense. The past tense is used to describe events that have already happened. The autobiographical passage below taken from an article called *B is for Bestseller* is by the author Mark Haddon, who also wrote a well known book about a boy with Asperger's Syndrome called *The Curious Incident of the Dog in the Night-Time*. Can you identify any examples of the past tense in this recount text?

I've been writing books for children for 17 years. Over that time, I've received a steady trickle of letters. Most are from readers telling me how much they've enjoyed this or that book of mine, which always gives me a glow for the rest of the day. Others begin: 'Dear Mr Haddon, We're doing Authors with Mrs Patel and I've been told to write to you', which is flattering, but not in quite the same way. … The best question I ever received came from a boy who asked whether I did much crossing out. I explained that most of my work consisted of crossing out and that crossing out was the secret of all good writing.

Three years ago, I wrote *The Curious Incident of the Dog in the Night-Time*, a novel set in Swindon about a teenage boy with Asperger's syndrome who discovers a murdered poodle on a neighbour's lawn. It was published in two identical editions with different covers, one for adults and one for teenagers. To my continuing amazement, it seems to have spread round the world like some particularly infectious rash.

6 Preparing an essay

You are learning:
- to sequence text logically and use topic sentences.

Half the success of an essay is in the structure. Topic sentences give clarity and purpose to your essay.

Activity 1

You are going to write an essay about the basketball star and TV personality Ade Adepitan for a magazine aimed at teenagers. The following two texts are written versions of oral texts: a speech made about him when he was given an honorary degree at Loughborough University and an interview with the sportsman.

1   Read Text A and Text B.

Text A

Ade Adepitan

Public Orator, Charlie Bethel presented the Honorary Graduand at the Degree Ceremony held on Monday 17 July at 10.30 a.m.

Chancellor, Vice Chancellor, Distinguished Guests, Graduands, Ladies and Gentlemen. It was an honour to accept the role of orator today for the recipient.

Ade Adepitan was born in Maryland, just outside Lagos, Nigeria in 1973. Ade was a bouncing baby boy. Sadly six months later he had contracted polio, but he survived this debilitating disease and three years later Ade and his family moved to Britain and made their home in Newham, London.

Whilst at school Ade gave up the calipers which helped him walk and picked up a basketball, having seen the Great Britain Wheelchair Basketball Team in action. Since then he has never looked back. Ade has competed on every continent and at every level. He played professionally in Spain for two years for Zaragossa and he has taken up presenting. Ade's television debut was again as a dancing wheelchair user for Play Station and since then you may have seen him on *Sportsround*, *Tiger Tiger*, *Xchange*, and *Holiday*.

Television has allowed Ade to help those less fortunate than himself and he has campaigned against racism and disability discrimination as well as being a patron for Scope and the Association for Wheelchair Children.

In 2005 Ade was honoured by the Queen for services to Disability Sport following his efforts that saw Great Britain win the bronze at the Athens Summer Paralympic Games. The highlight of the Games for everyone in wheelchair basketball was the quarter final against the World Champions, USA. With his shoulder hurting and thousands in the arena watching, let alone the home crowd on the BBC, Ade made the baskets. With possession it saw GB progress to the semi-finals and finally win the bronze.

A more important achievement of Ade's to us was again in a team, in Singapore, on the 6th July 2005. An ambassador for London 2012, Ade was one of those beige-suited delegates sitting in front of Jacques Rogue as we all saw the Summer Olympic and Paralympic Games coming home. For Ade, his road to the Paralympics began at school when he had the opportunity to watch the then GB Wheelchair Basketball Team. Ade has become the role model for many youngsters, and an ambassador for sport, and the cycle has come full circle. Now we see many new athletes coming into sport thanks to him.

Chancellor, I have the honour to present to you and the University Adedoyin Olayiwola Adepitan MBE for the Degree of Doctor of the University *honoris causa*.

Public orator: Charlie Bethal

Text B

File   Edit   View   Favorites   Tools   Help

Address

Ade Adepitan – wheelchair basketball

Not only is Ade Adepitan a CBBC presenter, he's also an international wheelchair basketball player. At the Athens Paralympics in 2004 Ade was part of the Great Britain team that won the bronze medal.

How did you first get involved in wheelchair basketball?

Two physiotherapists contacted my school and asked me if I was interested in wheelchair sports. At the time I was using callipers (leg braces), and they asked me if I'd like to go to the Junior Wheelchair Games. I didn't really want to get into a wheelchair because I didn't think it was cool, but when I saw the Great Britain wheelchair basketball team training, I saw how cool they looked and how wicked their chairs were and I thought, 'this is the sport for me'.

What do you think is good about wheelchair basketball?

I like the competitiveness, the speed and the aggression. You've got to be physically fit, you've got to be strong, and you've also got to be intelligent, because you have to understand the plays.

What has been the greatest moment of your career so far?

Achievement-wise it's got to be winning the silver medal at the World Championships in Kitakyushu in Japan. Just playing in the final of the World Championships was just – I can't even explain it! Words can't explain what it's like!

Are there any other sports you enjoy?

Yeah, I'm a sports fanatic! I love watching football – I used to play football when I was younger. I'm not bad at tennis and I'm also into scuba diving – I love that! If it's an action sport where there is a lot of hard work and adrenalin involved then I'm into it.

Who are your sporting heroes?

Well, Muhammad Ali is my number one – he changed so much in boxing and he changed so much for black people as well. There's also Michael Jordan, who is the greatest basketball player that ever lived! It will be a long time before someone reaches the level that he has taken basketball to.

2 Select six headings from the list below to use as section headings for your essay plan.

> Childhood
> Sporting achievements
> How he became interested in basketball
> Charitable work
> The 2005 Athens Paralympic Games
>
> Hobbies and interests
> CBBC presenting
> TV work
> His personality
> Family

3 Write two or three bullet points summarising what you will include under each heading.

Activity 2

1 Which paragraph would you use at the beginning of your essay, following your introduction? Why?

2 Which four of the sections above did you **not** include in your plan? Why?

Activity 3

Read this magazine article introduction by another student.

1 Rewrite the text, correcting any errors in sentence structure, punctuation and spelling.

2 The first line is chatty and informal, to appeal to young people. Improve the tone of the rest of the piece to appeal to a teenage reader.

So how many of you dream of being a sporting hero? Ade Adepitan has achieved significant success in his career even though he is in a wheelchair, he is an example to young people of determination and self-belief. Despite the many prejudices he faced as a child because of his disability, he is famous for his sporting achievments and also as a tellyvision presenter.

Activity 4

A topic sentence in a text expresses the main idea of a paragraph. It is usually the first sentence of the paragraph.

Below is a plan for an essay on Ade Adepitan's life. Write a topic sentence to begin each paragraph, based on your reading. The first one has been done for you.

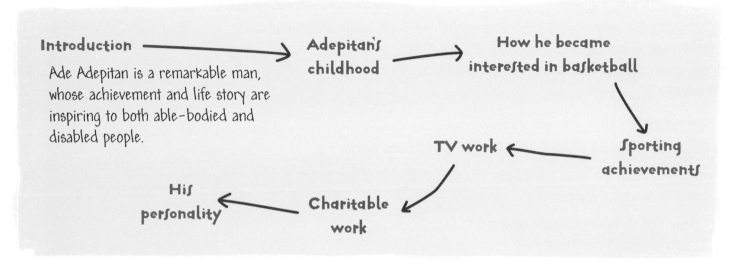

Introduction

Ade Adepitan is a remarkable man, whose achievement and life story are inspiring to both able-bodied and disabled people.

Adepitan's childhood

How he became interested in basketball

Sporting achievements

TV work

Charitable work

His personality

Assess your progress

The success criteria for this section were:
- selecting topics to form an essay plan
- writing bullet points against these topics
- justifying your choices.

Discuss activities 1 and 2 on pages 18–20 with a partner.
1 Which of the success criteria did you find difficult, and why?
2 Which of the success criteria did you find easy, and why?

Sharpen your skills Adverbs

- an adverb tells us more about a verb, an adjective or an adverb
- an adverb can tell us how, when, where or why
- adverbs often end in -ly.

Re-read paragraph 5 of text A, on page 18. Then rewrite the paragraph, adding three appropriate adverbs to the passage. Add them to the verbs to emphasise how much the reader should admire Adepitan's charitable work.

Assessment task

Steve Irwin, Crocodile Hunter

Steve Irwin is well known for his work with crocodiles and other animals. In 2006, he was stung by a bull ray fish and died.

You have been asked to do some research about Steve Irwin, for a book about people who are well known for their work with animals. You have been given various texts about Steve Irwin which you can use for your research.

Your task

Look at texts A–E on pages 22-9 and do the activities below.

1 Skim through the texts and briefly explain what kind of text each one is and how you can tell.

2 Scan text C. Find and write down:
   a Two facts about Steve Irwin.
   b Two opinions about Steve Irwin.

3 a Say which text you think is going to be **most** helpful to you and explain why.
   b Say which text is going to be **least** helpful to you and explain why.

4 Choose one text which you think presents Steve Irwin in either a **positive** or a **negative** way and explain how the text does this. In your answer, comment on:
   ● the choice of information included about Steve Irwin
   ● the choice of language used to describe him and what he did
   ● other techniques used to convey a particular view of Steve Irwin.

5 What impression do you get of Steve Irwin as a person from the texts? Support your answer with quotations from at least two of them.

6 Make notes of the main points you want to include in your biography of Steve Irwin, and organise them into paragraphs. You can decide whether you want to present him in a positive or a negative way – or present a balanced point of view about him. You can decide how you want to organise your notes.

Text A

Daredevil Irwin dies doing what he loved best

CAIRNS, Australia – Wildlife warrior Steve Irwin was a daredevil who loved flirting with danger around deadly animals.

But after years of close shaves it was a normally harmless stingray which finally claimed his life on Monday, plunging a barb into the Crocodile Hunter's chest as he snorkelled in shallow water on the Great Barrier Reef.

The 44-year-old TV personality may have died instantly when struck by the stingray while filming a sequence for his eight-year-old daughter Bindi's new TV series, friends believe.

'You think about all the documentaries we've made and all the dangerous situations that we have been in, you always think "is this it, is this a day that may be his demise?",' said his friend

> **"He died doing what he loved best."**

and manager John Stainton. '[But] nothing would ever scare Steve or would worry him. He didn't have a fear of death at all."

Mr Irwin made his international reputation wrestling crocodiles and snakes. But the flamboyant naturalist's final confrontation with a wild animal occurred at Batt Reef off Port Douglas on Monday morning, where he had been filming a new documentary, *Ocean's Deadliest*.

Taking time off from the main project, Mr Irwin was swimming in shallow water, snorkelling as his cameraman filmed large bull rays.

'He came over the top of a stingray and the stingray's barb went up and went into his chest and put a hole into his heart,' said Mr Irwin's friend and manager John Stainton.

'It's likely that he possibly died instantly when the barb hit him, and I don't think that he ... felt any pain.'

Wildlife experts said the normally passive creatures only sting in defence, striking with a bayonet-like barb when they feel threatened.

Unconscious, Mr Irwin was pulled aboard his research vessel, *Croc One*, for a 30-minute dash to Low Isle, where an emergency helicopter had been summoned at about 11 a.m., his Australia Zoo said in a statement.

The crew of the *Croc One* performed constant CPR during the voyage to Low Isle, but medical staff pronounced Mr Irwin dead about noon.

His wife Terri was told of her husband's death while on a walking tour in Tasmania, and returned to the Sunshine Coast with her two children, Bindi and three-year-old son Bob.

The death of the larger than life Mr Irwin, best known for his catchcry 'Crikey!', caused shockwaves around the world, leading TV bulletins in the United States and Britain.

Mr Irwin was also a global phenomenon, making almost 50 documentaries which appeared on the cable TV channel Animal Planet, and which generated books, interactive games and even toy action figures.

Prime Minister John Howard said: 'I am quite shocked and distressed at Steve Irwin's sudden, untimely and freakish death. It's a huge loss to Australia.

'He was a wonderful character. He was a passionate environmentalist. He brought joy and entertainment and excitement to millions of people.'

"He was one of Australia's best known personalities internationally and an ambassador for the nation and its wildlife."

The Melbourne-born father of two's *Crocodile Hunter* programme was first broadcast in 1992 and has been shown around the world on cable network Discovery.

He also starred in movies and helped develop the Australia Zoo wildlife park, north of Brisbane, which was started by his parents Bob and Lyn Irwin.

He grew up near crocodiles, trapping and removing them from populated areas and releasing them in his parents' park, which he took over in 1991.

Bob was involved in a controversial incident in January 2004, when his father held his infant son in one arm as he fed a dead chicken to a crocodile at Australia Zoo.

Child-welfare and animal-rights groups criticised his actions as irresponsible and tantamount to child abuse.

Mr Irwin said any danger to his son was only a perceived danger and that he was in complete control of the situation.

In June 2004, Mr Irwin came under fire again when it was alleged he came too close to and disturbed some whales, seals and penguins while filming a documentary in Antarctica.

Mr Irwin was also a tourism ambassador and was heavily involved in last year's 'G'Day LA' tourism campaign.

Queensland Premier Peter Beattie said Mr Irwin was an 'extraordinary man'.

'He has made an enormous difference to his state and his country,' he said.

Sydney Morning Herald
4 September 2006

Text C

STEVE WASN'T GOING TO DIE IN BED

BY VIRGINIA WHEELER
5 SEPTEMBER 2006

Irwin, wife Terri and a croc

WILDLIFE expert David Bellamy last night told of his grief at the loss of Crocodile Hunter Steve Irwin – but said: 'He was never going to die quietly in his bed.'

The British botanist called Aussie icon Irwin – killed by a stingray while snorkelling yesterday – a 'fantastic all-action character'.

He said: 'I had a good cry when I heard the terrible news. Why did it happen to such an important and talented guy? It is the world's loss and has sadly come years too early.'.

Outrageous Irwin, 44, won global TV fame by leaping on the backs of giant crocodiles and grabbing deadly snakes while crowing in a broad Aussie accent: 'Crikey! Look at this little bewdy.'

Though one of the world's top naturalists, many of his millions of fans feared he would eventually be killed taking one chance too many with a croc.

But he died while filming a bull ray in shallow water at Batt Reef, a remote part of the Great Barrier Reef in northern Queensland.

The 5ft-wide ray, normally a placid creature, suddenly turned on him and speared him through the heart with a lash from the toxic barb on its tail.

A plume of blood filled the crystal-clear reef water. And dad-of-two Irwin – universally loved for his childlike enthusiasm, khaki shorts and huge boots – died almost instantly.

Last night it was unclear if he was killed by the wound, a heart attack, poison from the blade-like barb or a combination of all three.

Paramedics tried in vain to revive him and he was pronounced dead on his boat, Croc One.

His death was caught on film by a cameraman from his production company, who was swimming in front of him.

The footage was being studied by police last night. Irwin always told film crews to keep shooting even if it looked like he was going to come off worst in a croc or shark attack.

His best friend and manager John Stainton, who witnessed the tragedy, wept as he said: 'Steve would have been sad if he died and it wasn't captured on camera.

'He died doing what he loved best and left this world in a happy and peaceful state of mind. I hope he never felt any pain. The world has lost a great wildlife icon, a passionate conservationist and one of the proudest dads on the planet.

'His last words would have been, "Crocs rule!"'

Irwin's American wife Terri, daughter Bindi, eight, and son Bob, three, were on holiday in Tasmania when they learned of his death.

They flew to Queensland last night and headed for the family home at Minyama on the state's Sunshine Coast.

Text D

In late October 2000, writer Sarah Simpson from magazine *Scientific American* finds herself seated at a table in Steve Irwin's childhood home. The Crocodile Hunter himself sits across from her, explaining how his father built this house in 1970. Now it has become one of the administrative buildings for Australia Zoo, which Irwin's parents established and which he now directs together with his wife, Terri.

SCIENTIFIC AMERICAN: Why do you think you're so popular?

STEVE: Nothing to do with my looks, that's for sure! [laughing] Yeah, I normally get a big croc out in the foreground of any filming.

You know what I reckon it is? My belief is that what comes across on the television is a capture of my enthusiasm and my passion for wildlife. Since I was a boy, from this house, I was out rescuing crocodiles and snakes. My mum and dad were very passionate about that and, I was lucky enough to go along. The first crocodile I ever caught was at nine years of age, and it was a rescue. So now what happens is the cameras follow me around and capture exactly what I've been doing since I was a boy. Only now we have a team of, you know, like 73 of us, and it's gone beyond that.

As the audience, I want you to come with me, right? So we get cameras, every one of us, if we've got a four- or five-man film crew, including myself and Terri. Every one of us can use a camera. I have one in my green backpack that I pull out for the hard-core shots where you've gotta get right in there, so the camera's always right there, in there, while I'm doing my thing. So when I'm talking to the camera, I'm talking to *you*, in your living room.

We've evolved from sitting back on our tripods and shooting wildlife films like they have been shot historically, which doesn't work for us. So, now it's not just, 'Oh look, there's a cheetah making a kill.' I want to take you to the cheetah. I want to get in there as close as I can to that cheetah. You'll see me in Namibia getting attacked by a female cheetah, because I didn't know she had cubs, but the cameras are right there in a four-wheel-drive, filming me. She's 'grrraagh!' putting mock-charges on, and you get that overwhelming sensation that you're there, that you're with me.

SA: And what do you think your zany attitude does for the viewers?

STEVE: It excites them, which helps me to educate. I believe that education is all about being excited about something. Seeing passion and enthusiasm helps push an educational message. That's the main aim in our entire lives – to promote education about wildlife and wilderness areas, save habitats, save endangered species, etc. So, if we can get people excited about animals, then by crikey, it makes it a heck of a lot easier to save them.

My field is with apex predators, hence your crocodiles, your snakes, your spiders. And then of course you've got lions, tigers, bears. Great big apex predators – they're the species that I enjoy the most. That's where my passion lies. Historically, people have seen them as evil, ugly monsters that kill people. Take the crocodile, for example, my favourite animal. There are 23 species. Seventeen of those species are rare or endangered. They're on the way out, no matter what anyone does or says, you know.

So, my tactic with conservation of apex predators is to get people excited and take them to where they live.

The real crocodile hunter

By Germaine Greer
5 September 2006

Irwin tosses chicken to a crocodile while holding his baby son.

The world mourns. World-famous wildlife warrior Steve Irwin has died a hero, doing the thing he loved, filming a sequence for a new TV series. He was supposed to have been making a new documentary to have been called *Ocean's Deadliest*, but, when filming was held up by bad weather, he decided to 'go off and shoot a few segments' for his eight-year-old daughter's upcoming TV series. His manager John Stainton 'just said fine, anything that would keep him moving and keep his adrenaline going.' Evidently it's Stainton's job to keep Irwin pumped larger than life, shouting 'Crikey!' and punching the air.

Irwin was the real Crocodile Dundee, a great Australian, an ambassador for wildlife, a global **phenomenon**. The only creatures he couldn't dominate were parrots. A parrot once did its best to rip his nose off his face.

What seems to have happened is that Irwin and a cameraman went off in a little dinghy to see what they could find. What they found were stingrays. You can just imagine Irwin yelling: 'Just look at these beauties! Crikey! With those barbs a stingray can kill a horse!' All Australian children know that stingrays bury themselves in the sand or mud with only their eyes sticking out. What you don't do with a stingray is stand on it. The lashing response of the tail is automatic; the barb is coated with a deadly slime.

As a Melbourne boy, Irwin should have had a healthy respect for stingrays. The film-makers maintain that the ray that took Irwin out was a 'bull ray', but this is not usually found as far north as Port Douglas. **Marine biologist** Dr Meredith Peach has been quoted as saying, 'It's really quite unusual for divers to be stung unless they are grappling with the animal and, knowing Steve Irwin, perhaps that may have been the case.'

The only time Irwin ever seemed less than entirely lovable to his fans (as distinct from **zoologists**) was when he went into the Australia Zoo crocodile enclosure with his month-old baby son in one hand and a dead chicken in the other. For a second you didn't know which one he meant to feed to the crocodile. If the crocodile had been less depressed it might have made the decision for him. As the dozy beast obediently downed its tiny snack, Irwin walked his baby on the grass, not something that **paediatricians** recommend for rubbery baby legs even when there isn't a stir-crazy carnivore a few feet away. The adoring world was momentarily appalled. They called it child abuse. The whole spectacle was revolting.

Irwin's response to the sudden outburst of criticism was bizarre. He believed that he had the crocodile under control. But he could have fallen over, suggested an interviewer. He admitted that was possible, but only if a meteor had hit the earth and caused an earthquake of 6.6 on the **Richter scale**.

What Irwin never seemed to understand was that animals need space. The one lesson any conservationist must try to drive home is that habitat loss is the principal cause of species loss. There was no habitat, no matter how fragile or finely balanced, that Irwin hesitated to barge into. There was not an animal he was not prepared to manhandle. Every creature he brandished at the camera was in distress. Every snake badgered by Irwin was at a huge disadvantage, with only a single possible reaction to its terrifying situation, which was to strike. But Irwin was an entertainer, a 21st-century version of a lion-tamer, with crocodiles instead of lions.

Explanations

phenomenon **remarkable person**
Marine biologist **scientist who studies the sea**
zoologists **scientists who study animals**
paediatricians **doctors of children's diseases**
Richter scale **measurement scale for earthquakes named after its creator Dr Charles F. Richter**

Assessment task
Writing: Composition and conventions

Steve Irwin, a biography

Your task

You have been asked to write a biography of Steve Irwin. You have read and studied texts about him and made some notes. If you like, you can include some information and opinions from other material you find yourself. You can choose whether you present him in a positive way or a negative way – or present a balanced point of view about him.

You should:

- organise your points logically into paragraphs or sections with subheadings and provide an effective beginning and ending

- use a variety of sentence structures and remember to link your ideas using a range of connectives

- use capital letters, full stops and commas accurately to make your writing clear for the reader.

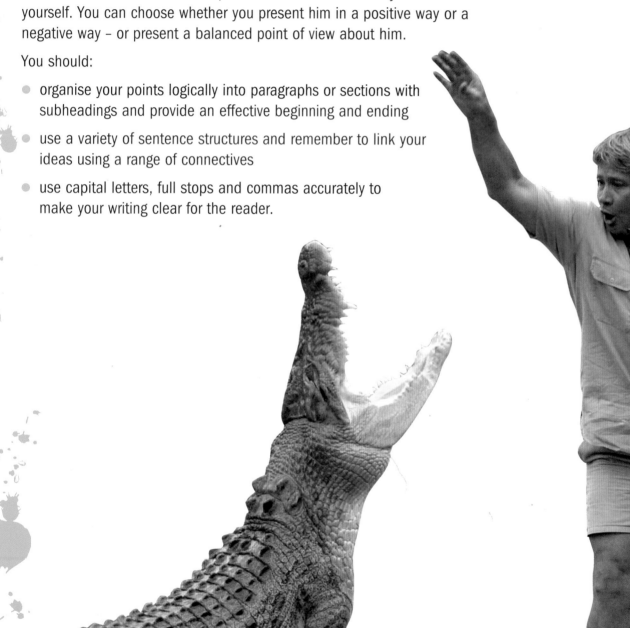

2 News

Objectives

In this unit you will:

Reading
- use skimming and scanning to find information in a text
- infer and deduce the meaning of a text
- recognise and comment on how writers' choices have an effect on readers
- explore how the structure and presentation of a text help to create meaning.

Composition
- plan and develop a written argument
- use evidence and opinions to develop your own point of view
- use punctuation between sentences accurately to make meaning clear
- use apostrophes accurately.

Speaking and Listening
- present a talk in which the structure and vocabulary make your ideas clear
- work with others to develop a role-play.

Language
- understand and use the terms 'noun phrase' and 'verb phrase'.

By the end of this unit you will:
- present a news story (Speaking and Listening: Drama role-play and performance).
- read and answer questions on a news article (Reading: Reading for meaning)

Cross-curricular links

- **ICT**
  Communicating information
- **Citizenship**
  Advocacy and representation

1 Presenting the news

You are learning:

- what makes the news, the different forms it takes, and how we choose to get it.

The news is all around us. Events and incidents are always happening and the news is being updated constantly.
A hundred years ago the only way to get the news was by reading a newspaper; today, people can access the news when and how they want it.

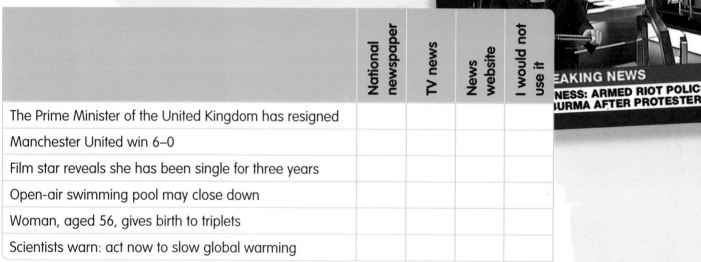

Activity 1

1 Which of the stories in the table below would you put in a national newspaper, television news report or news website? Which would you not use at all?

	National newspaper	TV news	News website	I would not use it
The Prime Minister of the United Kingdom has resigned				
Manchester United win 6–0				
Film star reveals she has been single for three years				
Open-air swimming pool may close down				
Woman, aged 56, gives birth to triplets				
Scientists warn: act now to slow global warming				

2 **a** Which of the stories in question 1 did you include in all three media: the newspaper, the television news and the news website?

   b Which stories did you not include in all three? Why not?

3 Write a sentence beginning 'News is …', in which you explain the kind of information we can get from newspapers, television news and news websites.

Activity 2

1 Different media present the news in different ways for different people. What are the advantages and disadvantages of newspapers, television news and news websites? Think about:
- how and when people can access them
- how much news they provide
- how much the reader or viewer can choose which stories to find out about.

2 Which media – television news, newspaper or news website – would you recommend for Jemima, Derek, Chris and Carrie?

I'm very busy. The only time I can catch up on the news is in taxis or on trains. I'm mainly interested in financial and political news.

Jemima

We want a quick summary of all the news after the kids are in bed but we're usually too tired to read by then.

Chris and Carrie

I want to know everything that's going on. I can spend hours finding out all about the latest stories and events in the world.

Derek

3 Look carefully at the images on page 32. They are from *Sky News, The Times* newspaper and the *Telegraph* website.

How would you describe the newsreader and the newsroom, the newspaper front page and the news website? Why have they been presented in this way?

Sharpen your skills – Noun and verb phrases

Noun phrases are groups of words which include a noun (the head or most important word) and others which add information to it. In this sentence, the noun phrases are underlined and the headwords have been circled: 'The large (dog) wagged its shaggy brown (tail).'

1 Copy these sentences then underline the noun phrases and circle the headwords.

  a An old grey-haired man walked slowly towards the small corner shop.

  b The best day I can remember was when we went to the largest theme park in Florida.

The verb in a sentence is called the verb phrase. Sometimes these contain more than one verb: the main verb and one or more auxiliary verbs. The verb phrase in this sentence has been underlined; the main verb has been circled: 'I am (going) to bed.'

2 Copy these sentences then underline the verb phrase and circle the main verb.

- Mum had cooked a large roast dinner.
- The sprouts had been boiled for an hour and a half.
- No one would eat them.

2 Features of a newspaper front page

You are learning:

- to explore the layout of a newspaper front page and to write an effective headline.

The front page of a newspaper needs to be bold and eyecatching. It uses distinct features to achieve this.

Activity 1

Masthead
The name and logo of the newspaper

Puff
An eye-catching graphic to advertise what else can be found inside the newspaper

Headline
Sums up the main newspaper story to attract and intrigue the reader

Image
A picture to illustrate the article

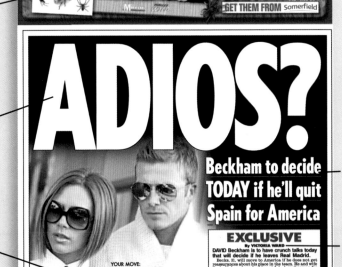

Strapline
Adds a little more detail to the headline

Byline
Tells the reader who wrote the article

Text
The main body of the article, telling the story in detail

1 Which of these layout features:
   a Clearly and boldly shows the name of the newspaper?
   b Tempts the reader to buy the newspaper with things on offer inside?
   c Encourages the reader to read the story on the front page by summing it up in as few words as possible?
   d Adds a little more detail to the headline?
   e Says who wrote the article?
   f Illustrates the subject of the story?
   g Gives more detailed information, including facts and quotes?

Explanations

Adios **Spanish for goodbye**

Activity 2

An effective headline should sum up the news story and attract the reader's attention, making them want to find out more.

1 Look at the headline for the news story on page 34. Write down two or more reasons to explain why you think the headline writer chose it.

2 Here are some rules for effective headline writing. A good headline:
- summarises the story in as few words as possible
- leaves out unnecessary words like 'the' or 'a'
- is often written in the present tense
- often uses dramatic or *emotive* language
- sometimes uses a play on words or *pun*
- sometimes uses *alliteration*: two or more words beginning with the same sound or letter.

Which rules do these headlines follow?

A FOWL PLAY, REF

12/05/2007

TWO chickens are so addicted to football they have learnt to dribble, slide-tackle and do headers in their yard in China.

B SPIDERS IN BOY'S EAR

08/05/2007

A BOY who complained of a popping noise in his head 'like Rice Krispies' had two spiders living in his ear canal.

C MOBILES ARE KILLING OFF BEES

By Victoria Ward 16/04/2007

MOBILE phones have killed millions of bees, scientists said last night. The radiation is said to interfere with their navigation systems which prevents them finding their way back to hives.

D CASE CAT'S PLANE ADVENTURE

By Mirror.co.uk 03/05/2007

A Canadian cat has inadvertently become a jet-setter after sneaking into a suitcase before her owner flew off for a business trip.

Activity 3

1 Use the table below to help you select the best words to create the most effective headline for this story.

A school is so infested with rats, they are invading classrooms during lessons and frightening students.

rat	infested	school	frightens	students
rodent	filled	lessons	terrifies	pupils
animal	riddled	classroom	scares	children

2 Which of the rules for writing effective headlines have you used? Write two or three sentences explaining how you have made your headline effective.

Assess your progress

1 Design a newspaper front page for the headline you wrote in Activity 3. Remember to include all the features you explored in Activity 1.

2 Write a list of all the features you have included in your front page.

3 Write a sentence or two for each feature, explaining the effect you were trying to create.

Structure of a newspaper

You are learning:
- how the information in a newspaper article is organised by exploring the structure of an article and planning your own.

A newspaper article isn't just a story, it's a carefully crafted information text, with its own style and particular use of language.

Activity 1

Read this newspaper story then answer the questions to help you understand how the information in the article has been organised.

Boy gets toilet seat stuck on his head

Firefighters said on Wednesday they had come to a boy's rescue after he got a toilet seat stuck on his head.

The toddler, aged two-and-a-half, and his mother walked into a fire station in Braintree, Essex on Tuesday saying the boy had put his head through a small trainer seat for the toilet and now could not remove it.

'His mum had tried to get it over his head but couldn't budge it so she walked him down here and asked us to have a look at it and we went to work and we managed to get it off in no time,' firefighter Chris Cox said.

'We simply put some dishwashing liquid on his head and ears and it slid off nice as pie.'

He said the boy had been 'very brave' and 'toddled away as happy as can be' after his ordeal ended.

1 Write down:
   - **who** was involved
   - **when** it happened
   - **why** it happened.
   - **what** happened
   - **where** it happened

2 Which paragraphs give you all this information?

3 What information do the other paragraphs give?

4 Why has the writer included quotations from the firefighter?

5 How many sentences are there in each paragraph? Why do you think the writer has done this?

6 Write a set of instructions on structuring a newspaper article. Use these sentence starters to help you.
   - The first one or two paragraphs of a newspaper article should tell the reader …
   - The middle paragraphs of a newspaper article should …
   - The writer often includes quotations to …
   - The final paragraph of a newspaper article usually …
   - The number of sentences in each paragraph can vary but often …

Activity 2

You are a newspaper reporter. You have been given the following information and told to write an article for tomorrow's front page.

Follow the steps below to prepare a role-play in which you will interview the key characters to find out the facts of the case.

International pop star, Buster Bling, has been arrested. The police say he is accused of stealing his girlfriend's pet budgie. His girlfriend is called Donna Bellissimo. The budgie's name is Derek.

17366

1 Decide which characters you will interview. You should talk to Buster Bling, Donna Bellissimo and the police. You could also interview Buster's solicitor or even get a budgie expert's comments.

2 Before you begin your interviews, you need to plan what each character is like, what they know and what they think. Use the points below to help you.

   a Write down two or three words to describe the personality and attitudes of each character in the story.
   b Write a short biography – two or three sentences – for each character.
   c What do they think of the other people involved?
   d What were they doing at the time the budgie went missing?
   e Why do they think this might have happened?

3 Plan the questions you will ask your interviewees, then plan their answers.

4 Rehearse and perform your role-play.

Remember: the most important thing in a role-play is to sustain, or keep up, your role. Don't laugh or stop being the character you are playing. What would you think if a film actor did that in the middle of a movie?!

Activity 3

The editor of your newspaper wants the Buster Bling story on the front page with a large headline and a big picture of Buster. You have only six paragraphs to write your Buster Bling story. What will you put in each paragraph? Use the instructions you wrote in Activity 1 to help you plan the structure of your article.

4 Aiming at a target audience

You are learning:
- how newspaper stories are chosen to suit their readers and how different newspapers tell the same stories in different ways.

Local newspapers are full of local news, aimed at local readers. They don't usually include the national news – politics, international affairs, major sporting events – unless they have something to do with the area in which the local newspaper is sold.

Activity 1

1 Which do you think these headlines might have been taken from – local or national newspapers?

A **Ice rink to re-open before Christmas**

E **Ten new jobs at biscuit factory**

B **Rugovian president to meet Brown at No.10**

F **More Britons buying holiday homes abroad than ever before**

C *Thousands of bank notes could be forgeries*

G **New toys for toddler playgroup**

D **Chelsea win again – and again**

H **Community police officer retires after thirty years' service**

2 Choose four of these headlines – two from a local newspaper and two from a national newspaper. Write an explanation of how you decided which kind of newspaper they were from.

Activity 2

Here are the headlines and opening paragraphs of two articles from two national newspapers. They tell the same story but are written in very different ways. Answer the questions to explore the differences and how the newspapers aim for different audiences.

Welcome to Modbury. Just don't ask for a plastic bag

Modbury is the **quintessential** small West Country town. Set in a hollow among rolling Devon hills just a few miles from the sea, it has 760 households, a high street, three churches, a primary school, several pubs, two takeaways, a surgery, a small supermarket and 40 or so small shops.

Not much happens in Modbury. Some say the last time the peace was disturbed was in 1643 when Roundheads and Cavaliers fought in its streets. But a revolution of another kind will take place on Monday. At 8 a.m. it will become the first plastic bag-free town in Europe.

Guardian

TOWN AXES PLASTIC BAGS

A MARKET town is banning all plastic bags from tomorrow. In a trailblazing move shoppers in Modbury, Devon, will be provided with **biodegradable** cornstarch bags, recyclable paper bags or reusable cotton and jute bags. The scheme – believed to be the first of its kind in Europe – is being joined by all the town's 43 traders – from family shops to the local supermarket.

Daily Mirror

Explanations

quintessential **typical, a perfect example**
biodegradable **decomposes and rots over time, so less harmful to the environment**

1 Write a summary of this story in one sentence.

2 Look again at the first paragraph of each of the two articles:
   a Which one contains more information?
   b What kind of information does each one give?
   c What do you notice about the length of the paragraphs?

3 When do the two articles tell the reader the main point of the story?

4 The *Mirror* describes Modbury as 'a market town'. The *Guardian* describes it as 'the quintessential small West Country town'. What do you notice about the two newspapers' choice of language?

5 Compare the two articles' headlines. Would you describe their language as formal or informal? Which uses more emotive or dramatic language?

6 Write two or three sentences summing up the differences between these two articles.

7 What kind of readers do you think these two newspapers are trying to appeal to?

Sharpen your skills — Sentence types

There are four different sentence types:
Statement: a sentence that states a fact or an opinion and is either true or false. It ends with a full stop, for example, 'I like cheese.' or 'Three plus four makes seven.'
Question: a sentence that asks for a response. It ends with a question mark, for example, 'Are you ready yet?'
Command: a sentence that gives an instruction or makes a request. It can end with a full stop or an exclamation mark, for example: 'Sit down!' or 'Boil for ten minutes.'
Exclamation: a sentence used to express a strong feeling. It always ends with an exclamation mark, for example, 'Oh my goodness!' or 'Ouch!'

What kind of sentences are these?
- You should only cross the road at a zebra crossing.
- Can you be sure that a driver has seen you?
- Drivers never pay enough attention to pedestrians.
- Do you always do that?
- Be safe!
- Idiots!

5 Reading for meaning

You are learning:
- how to retrieve information by scanning for facts, identifying opinions and reading between the lines.

You are often asked to read a text and answer questions about it. An effective way of retrieving this information is to identify a key word in the question – a word which is important – and scan the text for it. This means you do not have to re-read the whole text – you can just look for the word you need to help you answer the question.

Activity 1

In question 1 below the key words are *crash diet*. Scan the article to find them. This will lead you to the answer.

The Labradors too fat to go for a walk

Flabradors Tasha and Heidi are being forced to go on a crash diet to save their lives – after ballooning to a whopping SEVEN stone each.

The plump pooches piled on the pounds by wolfing down 1000 grams of dog food a day – twice the recommended amount – on top of fatty snacks.

To make matters worse, the 10-year-old sisters were hardly ever walked by their last owner, who has recently signed them over to the RSPCA.

They are left panting and out of breath after just a few minutes on their paws and when they attempt to run or jump their coats ripple with fat.

Officers are so worried their hind legs will buckle under the huge bulk that they have put them on a strict weight-loss plan to get them down to the normal three-and-a-half stone.

Most Labradors live to the age of 14, but Tasha and Heidi may not reach that age because they are in such a poor state of health.

RSPCA Centre manager Nikki Smith said: 'We are saddened by the state of these dogs as it clearly shows they have not had the exercise they need for many months.

'With guidance from our vet they are given short spells of exercise in the centre dog run where they can be carefully monitored.

'But sadly unless they can shed a few pounds, they may not reach their full life span of 14 years because their weight does put extra strain on their hearts.

'We just want to remind dog owners that it's vital to keep an eye on their pets' health – and not kill them with kindness.'

1 Why have the dogs been put on a crash diet?

2 How much dog food were the dogs used to eating?

3 How often were the dogs walked by their last owner?

4 What is the normal weight for a Labrador?

5 What is the full life span for a Labrador?

Activity 2

A fact is something that can be proved to be true. An opinion is what someone thinks or believes – other people may disagree.

You shouldn't believe every word you read. You need to be able to tell the difference between what is true and what is just the writer's opinion.

1   Which of these statements taken from the article are facts and which
    are opinions?
    a   The dogs weigh seven stone.   c   The dogs will not live as long as they should.
    b   The dogs are ten years old.   d   The dogs are huge.

2   Write down three facts and three opinions about your school.

Activity 3

Sometimes the writer's opinion is not clearly stated. It is
suggested or *implied* by the words the writer uses. You need
to read between the lines to work out the writer's opinion.
Read this sentence from the article again:

> The plump pooches piled on the pounds by wolfing
> down 1000 grams of dog food a day – twice the
> recommended amount – on top of fatty snacks.

1   There are some facts in this sentence. What are they?

2   The writer adds his opinion to the facts through his choice of
    language. What do these words suggest or imply about the writer's
    opinion: *plump, piled on, wolfing, fatty*?

3   This sentence does not mention the dog's owner. Write a sentence
    using the same facts to suggest or imply the opinion that it is the
    owner's fault the dogs are overweight.

4   a   Write down three other words from the article which the writer
        has used to suggest this opinion.
    b   Are these words formal or informal?

5   What do these words suggest about the writer's attitude to this
    story? Does the writer think it is funny or worrying that the dogs
    are so overweight?

Assess your progress

How confident are you about the skills you have practised in these activities?
Assess yourself using the grid below.

	I can't do this ✓	I think I can do this ✓	I can definitely do this ✓
I can scan a text for key words and retrieve information			
I can identify facts			
I can identify opinions			
I can identify the writer's opinion implied by the words the writer chooses			
I can imply an opinion in my own writing through the words I choose			

6 Recounting events

You are learning:

● to explore a television news report and practise your recount skills.

Television news gives information in different ways from a newspaper. Differences in language, presentation and delivery mean the same story may end up creating very different responses from the two audiences.

Activity 1

Read the transcript of a news report and the newspaper article below, then answer the questions to help you explore television news.

Whale in the Thames report

News reporter:

Lost and alone, a long way from its usual waters, a northern bottlenose whale makes its way up the Thames through London. Usually a strong swimmer, this species is used to deep water much further north, not a tidal river like this.

Interviewee 1:

We've never seen an animal like this before. Our records at the museum go back to 1913 and this is the first record of this species in the Thames.

Whale stranded in Thames

Fears were growing for a whale that swam upstream in the Thames today, reaching central London after losing its way in the North Sea.

It is the first time since 1913 that a northern bottlenose whale has been seen in the Thames, and hundreds of onlookers rushed to the riverside to watch as it progressed past the Houses of Parliament.

Experts say they are very concerned for the whale – normally found in deep seawater – and there was increasing concern about its chances of making it back to the sea, around 40 miles downstream.

There was speculation that if it became beached and stranded it could have to be put down in a mercy killing to minimise its suffering.

At one stage before 2 p.m., the 4.5 metre (15 ft) long mammal came close to becoming beached near Battersea, coming within yards of the riverbank. A number of members of the public jumped into the river and splashed around to encourage the whale to move back into deeper waters.

It swam as far up river as Chelsea before lifeboats turned it around just short of Albert Bridge.

By 5 p.m. the whale – thought to be not yet fully grown – had moved away from the banks near Westminster and was spending more time beneath the surface.

Experts were at the scene, and a four-strong flotilla of boats – including a harbourmaster's vessel – kept watch on it.

Guardian

1 What are the main differences in the presentation and delivery of news in a newspaper article and a television news item?

2 Is the language used in this news report formal or informal? Write down two examples to support your answer.

3 What does this language suggest about the newsreader's opinion? Does the newsreader think it is funny or worrying that the whale is stranded?

4 How do the newsreader's voice and facial expressions help to express this opinion?

5 Try reading the transcript as if you were a newsreader, but using a different tone of voice to give a different opinion. What is the effect?

Activity 2

1 Re-read the news transcript. What are the key points of this story? Try to sum up the story in five short sentences, keeping all the important information. Remember: the key points of a news story are often Who, What, When, Why and Where.

2 Add one more key information point, making a total of six short sentences. Write a short explanation of why you chose that point.

3 Without looking, recount this story to a partner. Ask them to check you have included all the key information. Then swap roles.

Activity 3

The aim of this activity is to work in a group, helping each other to complete the task.

1 Choose a news headline from the suggestions here. Working in your group, make up the details of the story and prepare a brief recount of it for broadcast on television news. Remember: your viewers will want to know at least the five key points of the story: Who, What, When, Why and Where.

2 Write a short evaluation of your group work. Try to comment on:
   • how well you worked as a team
   • how you could help a group to work more effectively together next time.

Genius six-year-old beats world champion

Socks fetch record price on Internet auction

Teenage lottery winner buys school

Parrot foils burglars

School-trip teacher stranded on desert island for three years

Assessment task

Speaking and Listening: Drama, role-play and performance

The Hamster Story

You are a news team working for a local television company. You are given news stories and have to develop an item for the daily local television news which goes out at 6 p.m. You are given the news story below.

Lonely Hamster Does a Runner

Hammy, a 9-month-old hamster, escaped from his cage in Class 4 at Salt Edge Primary School during the half-term holiday. Caretaker Joe Smith discovered the school pet was missing on Thursday and had to break the news to tearful juniors who returned to school on Monday. 'First I knew was when I spotted the cage door was ajar,' said Mr Smith, 55, who has been caretaker at the school for 15 years.

Patsy Jones, teacher in charge of Class 4, claimed the cage had been securely shut when she left school the previous Friday. Hammy was supposed to be spending half-term with one of the children but in the rush to get away, Hammy was forgotten and so had to spend a lonely week on his own.

Local vet Pritesh Khan said: 'Hamsters are nervous creatures and you can't blame him for taking the opportunity to escape while he could.' This incident has raised the question of whether schools should be allowed to keep animals. Chris Jenkins of the local animal-rights group SAVE said 'This is exactly why people – and schools are included in this – should *not* be allowed to have pets. We are campaigning for keeping pets to be made illegal.'

However, child psychologist Sam Pepper told our reporter that looking after animals was one of the best ways of teaching children about responsibility. The debate goes on. Meanwhile, if you come across a hamster on the run, who can't find his way home, please phone our news desk on 01487 923710.

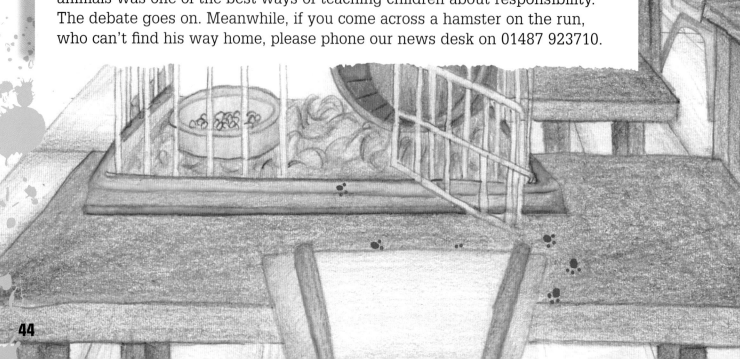

Joe Smith, the caretaker

Patsy Jones, Class 4 teacher

In your group you need:

- a newsreader
- a reporter at the scene of the escape
- an interviewer

You can include other people if you like.

Pritesh Khan, the local vet.

Chris Jenkins from SAVE

Your task

Create a news item for television based on this news story. You can decide the final format of your news story, but you should include as many of the following as possible:

- reporting the facts
- outside reporting from the scene of the escape
- interviews with people involved
- discussion with 'experts'
- comments from people in the street.

Sam Pepper, the child psychologist

If you are reading the news, interviewing or chairing a discussion, you can have some written questions to work from. Otherwise, you have to think beforehand what your character would think and feel and say. Try to:

- make each character different
- explore some of the issues raised by this story
- create an entertaining news item for the audience.

You will be assessed on:

- how well you work in a group, building on the ideas of other people to get the task done
- how well you listen to other people and show this in what you say
- how well you sustain your role in the news story.

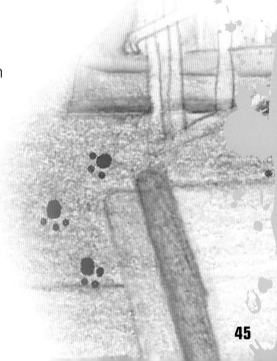

7 Point of view

You are learning:

- how writers express a point of view, developing your understanding of how language can imply an opinion.

In the same way that writers try to influence an audience by choosing which facts and opinions to give you, the careful use of words can subtly imply the opinion of the writer to try to influence you further.

Activity 1

1 Read the story.

Classroom thugs told: Disrupt school and win an iPod!

School tearaways are to be offered mountain bikes and iPods in return for good behaviour.

In a government campaign against soaring indiscipline, teachers are being told to reward disruptive pupils with prizes and privileges.

Badly-behaved youngsters must be praised five times as often as they are punished or criticised, under guidelines unveiled by Education Secretary Alan Johnson.

They can be offered prizes and privileges ranging from non-uniform days and extended breaktimes to CDs, cinema tickets, personal music players and state-of-the-art bicycles.

The scheme has been branded 'absurd'.

Ministers were accused of 'going soft' on discipline, and critics said the guidance would encourage pupils to expect prizes for good behaviour that should be considered the norm.

Chris Woodhead, the former chief inspector of schools, said: 'As a taxpayer, I would like to know how much this absurd guidance cost – it is a complete irrelevance to the real world.'

Tory education spokesman David Willetts said: 'Children have a very strong sense of fairness. It will be resented if it looks as if bad behaviour brings rewards.'

The new government advice states that pupils should be given five rewards for every criticism or punishment.

Minister's latest bright idea for curbing school thugs is to reward them.

'It has long been established that rewards are more effective than punishment in motivating pupils,' the guidelines say.

'By praising and rewarding positive behaviour, others will be encouraged to act similarly.'

Teachers are warned not to impose whole-class detentions or other sanctions that punish the innocent as well as the guilty'.

And they are told: 'Staff should also consider when it might be more appropriate, rather than impose a sanction, to encourage pupils to reflect on the harmful effects of their misbehaviour.'

The writer of this article does not openly state an opinion. You will have to read between the lines to work out the writer's point of view.

2 Write a summary of this story in two sentences. You could write about:
- what the government is suggesting
- what other people think about this.

3 It seems very clear what this news story is about.
a Compare the headline and the first sentence of the article. Complete these sentences to explain the difference:
- The headline says that children will be rewarded if …
- The first sentence says that children will be rewarded if …

b Is the headline wrong, or can you think of another reason why the headline writer might have done this?

4 Do you think the writer of this article thinks that the government's idea is a good one? Write down a quotation from the article that shows this.

Activity 2

1 Look at the caption for the photograph that accompanies this story.
a Why do you think the writer has chosen to describe badly behaved students as 'thugs'?
b The writer describes this new campaign as 'minister's latest bright idea'. What does the phrase 'bright idea' imply? What does the word 'latest' imply?

2 Why has the writer described indiscipline in schools as 'soaring'? What does it imply about behaviour in schools?

3 Count the number of words in the first five paragraphs.
a What do you notice about the length of the fifth paragraph?
b What effect is the writer aiming to achieve?
c How does the word 'absurd' contribute to this effect?

Activity 3

What do you think? Will this new idea make students behave better? Will it make good students behave badly? What do you think about whole-class detentions? What would be your policy to improve behaviour?

Write one or two paragraphs expressing your thoughts on improving behaviour in schools.

Activity 4

1 What are the key points the writer makes in the article on page 46? Read the article again and write them in a list. Use the first one here to get you started:

Key points

- School students are to be offered rewards to encourage good behaviour

-

-

2 What do you think? For each of the key points you identified in question 1, write a sentence or two which expresses your own point of view. You could set them out in a table like the one below. Remember: you may not agree with the example below – you need to express **your own** point of view.

Key points	My point of view
School students are to be offered rewards to encourage good behaviour	Anything that encourages good behaviour in schools must be good.

Activity 5

Look again at the points of view you wrote down in Activity 4, question 2. You are going to use them to write a letter to the newspaper that published the article on page 46. Your letter needs to respond to the writer's point of view and express your opinion.

To prepare for this task, complete the following questions.

1 When stating the writer's opinion, you can either put it in your own words or use quotations.
   a Write this quotation in your own words: 'Badly-behaved youngsters must be praised five times as often as they are punished or criticised.'
   b Write down a quotation that shows the different rewards pupils will be offered.

2 One way of structuring paragraphs in this kind of writing is to state the writer's opinion and then give your own point of view in response. For example:

The writer suggests that offering rewards for good behaviour is absurd. However, I believe schools should try anything that encourages students to behave.

Which word shows the link between these two opinions?

3   Once you have added your point of view to the writer's, you can go on to explain it further. Write a sentence that explains the point of view expressed in question 2: why is it so important that students behave well at school?

4   Now that you have explored how to structure and write your paragraphs, you are ready to write your letter. You could use the following structure:

Paragraph 1: Introduction – Why are you writing this letter?

Paragraph 2: Your first point – The writer's first key point; what you think about it.

Paragraph 3: Your second point – The writer's second key point; what you think about it.

Paragraph 4: Your third point – The writer's third key point; what you think about it.

Paragraph 5: Conclusion – Sum up your opinion and what you think should be done in the future to improve behaviour.

Remember: in paragraphs 2, 3 and 4, you can use the three-part structure you have already practised:
- the writer's opinion
- your opinion
- further explanation of your opinion.

Sharpen your skills Exclamation marks

There are three ways of showing the end of a sentence: a full stop, a question mark, or an exclamation mark. The exclamation mark is often used to make writing more like speech: it shows that the writer wants to emphasise a sentence, to say it forcefully.

Exclamation marks can also suggest a humorous tone. For example:

The trouble with exclamation marks is that people sometimes use too many of them. Read this. How many of the exclamation marks should be there, and how many would you edit out?

Stop it!

Be quiet!

I like dogs. But I couldn't eat a whole one!

My Cat!!
I love cats! They're so cool! They curl up on your lap and purr and fall asleep! They are the best pets in the world! My cat is called Barbara! Sometimes she catches birds and mice which is so disgusting! But most of the time she is really cute and I love her!

8 Bias

You are learning:

- how writers choose language and content to influence the reader's opinion.

Sometimes journalists give both sides of the story – a balanced point of view, the good and the bad, the 'for' and the 'against', the pros and the cons. And sometimes they don't.

Activity 1

1   Read this article and answer the questions to explore whose side the writer is on – and the content and language he has used to present it.

On trial for her life, the sausage dog who nipped a neighbour

By Paul Sims

A dangerous dog?

Lucy the sausage dog, a mere eight inches in height, doesn't look the most fearsome of creatures.

But the dachshund faces a death sentence under the Dangerous Dogs Act.

She has been accused of nipping a neighbour and her owner Melanie Hobson is to be tried for failing to keep her under control.

Yesterday Mrs Hobson, a full-time mother of two, spoke out in defence of Lucy.

'I can't believe this is happening,' she said. 'Lucy is a lovely dog and I would never have her round my kids if I thought she was dangerous.'

Mrs Hobson said that on 9 October, the day of the alleged attack, she was carrying shopping into her home at 3.45 p.m. while her children and three-year-old Lucy ran in front of her.

'Next thing I know, our neighbour accuses Lucy of biting him on the ankle. She's never done anything like that before.'

A week later, the police knocked on the door to take a statement from her.

'When they saw how big Lucy was, you could see in their faces they thought, "What are we doing here?" I thought that would be the last of it, but then I got the court summons and I was absolutely petrified.'

Mrs Hobson said she felt like a criminal when she appeared before Newcastle magistrates last week. She denied having a dog dangerously out of control in a public place.

'It was awful,' she said. 'I've never been to court before and I found it very intimidating. I'm not a criminal. On the face of it, it is funny – I mean, a sausage dog a dangerous dog? But then, the reality is I'm in court and the children could lose their best friend.'

She is due to stand trial in April and, if convicted, could be fined up to £5000 or jailed for up to six months.

Although a prison sentence is highly unlikely, the prospect of Lucy being destroyed is more than a possibility. Under the 1991 Dangerous Dogs Act certain breeds are specifically outlawed such as pit bull terriers.

However, Section 3 of the 1991 Act created an offence of being an owner of a dog of any type or breed which is dangerously out of control in a public place, or a non-public place in which it is not permitted to be.

Daily Mail

a Do you think that Lucy should be destroyed? Explain your answer in two or three sentences.

b Do you think the writer of this article thinks that Lucy should be destroyed? Explain your answer in two or three sentences.

c Is your opinion the same as the writer's? Do you think the writer has influenced your opinion with his choice of content and language?

2 For each of the following choices made by the writer, write a sentence explaining why you think he has made them:

a The writer only quotes the dog's owner. The neighbour does not give his side of the story.

b The writer describes the dog as 'a mere eight inches in height'.

c The writer uses the word 'nipped' to describe what the dog did to the neighbour.

d The writer says the dog 'faces a death sentence'.

e The writer quotes the mother saying, 'the children could lose their best friend'.

3 Match the following techniques of biased writing to the examples given in question 2 above:

a Statistics are used to back up the writer's opinion. Sometimes adjectives are added to emphasise the point being made, for example, 'More than a million people believe that ...'

b The writer tries to appeal to the reader's emotions making them feel, for example, sympathy or anger.

c Only one side of the argument is given. The opposition are not given the chance to present the other side.

d The writer chooses emotive language to exaggerate the point they are making.

Sharpen your skills Brackets

Add pairs of brackets to the following sentences to make their meanings clearer.

1 This pet or vicious attacker should die.

2 The dog really isn't dangerous maybe the victim is exaggerating.

3 The children's faces were full of sadness I hope they aren't going to cry thought their mother as she held them close.

Assess your progress

Create a poster showing some techniques that writers use in biased writing. For each technique, give a definition explaining the technique, and an example. You could use quotations from the article on page 50 as examples, or make them up.

9 Arguing a case

Writing to argue uses a lot of the same language techniques as biased writing. The purpose of an argument text, though, is to change the reader's opinion: to argue that the writer's opinion is the right one.

Activity 1

1 Read this article and think about how the writer has presented his point of view.

Are we really becoming more cruel to our pets?

In a week when the RSPCA reported a 77 per cent rise in animal abuse, TREVOR GROVE asks, are we really becoming more cruel to our pets?

The British are known all over the world as a nation of animal-lovers, and even mocked for it.

Yet now the RSPCA has come up with dismaying figures to suggest there has been a horrifying rise in cases of cruelty towards our fellow creatures in this country. Last year, the charity went to the aid of almost 100,000 dogs, cats, rabbits, guinea pigs and other animals – an increase of 77 per cent on the previous year.

Among the sickening incidents investigated by RSPCA inspectors was that of a woman who boiled her cat to death in the washing machine.

It must have struggled frantically to escape, as its claws were broken. In another case, a man used an electric carving knife to amputate one of his dog's legs, in order to save the vet's fee.

In 2005, the RSPCA received more than a million calls from worried members of the public. One can only guess at the amount of cruelty and neglect that is actually taking place but never gets reported.

Possibly the RSPCA is right and we have become a bit more careless. But have we really become more deliberately cruel? I suspect quite the opposite.

The very fact that the RSPCA is being besieged by so many reports from concerned members of the public is cause for hope – we are becoming more keenly aware when an animal is being mistreated and we are more eager to report it.

Yes, the growth of rescue organisations for dogs and cats shows that too many stupid, impatient or simply ill-prepared people are sadly prone to abandoning or mistreating pets.

But the very fact such bodies exist and successfully find new homes for thousands of pooches and pussies every year, surely suggests a heightened sense of responsibility towards the animals in our midst.

If the RSPCA sees more cases of cruelty towards animals, then that is certainly sad.

But we should not lose sight of the kindness shown towards most species, which is still a distinguishing feature of the British identity.

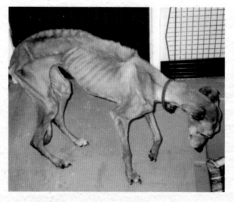 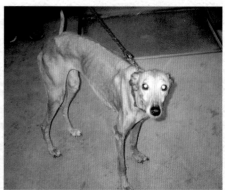

Meg was found starved and neglected. Now (pictured right) she has made a full recovery

Daily Mail

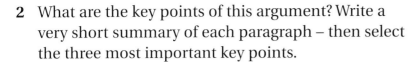

2   What are the key points of this argument? Write a very short summary of each paragraph – then select the three most important key points.

3   Write down one fact from this article. Why do you think the writer included it?

4   Write down one opinion from this article. Why do you think the writer included it?

5   Which of the following techniques that you found in biased writing can you spot in this article?
    • statistics   • emotive language   • emotional appeal.
    Write down an example of each from the text.

6   The writer of this article uses other language techniques to present his argument. Read the definitions of these below, then try to find at least one example of each.

- **Rhetorical questions:** the writer asks the reader a question to involve them in the argument.
- **Examples:** facts or stories used as evidence to prove a point in the argument.
- **A list:** used to emphasise a point.

- **Crushing a counter argument:** the other side of the argument is given, and then shown to be wrong.
- **First person:** 'I' is used to present opinions; 'we' is used to involve and engage the reader in the argument.

Sharpen your skills   Apostrophes of possession

Read this sentence: The girl's socks were blue.
The apostrophe plus the 's' mean the girl owns the socks. 'Girl' is the *owner word*. When showing something belonging to someone, the apostrophe goes at the end of the *owner word*, before the 's'.

Owner + ' + s thing = the thing belongs to its owner

Write down three more examples using apostrophes to show belonging or possession. Start with this one: The dog's tail.

Things get slightly more complicated when the word is plural. Remember: the apostrophe goes at the end of the owner word; you don't need to add an 's' if the word already ends in 's'.
So if you were writing about two tails belonging to two dogs, or lots of tails belonging to lots of dogs, you would write: The dogs' tails. Now read this:

A boy fell out of a tree. Unfortunately he landed on his friend. I thought that both the boy's arms were broken. It was worse than I thought. Both the boys' arms were broken.

Find the two apostrophes in these sentences. Then explain what happened.

Assessment task

Tuesday 7 November 2006

Take a last look

Photo: Johnnathan Hayward/AP

Polar bears play on the tundra near Churchill, Manitoba, Canada, November 2006

They are one of our most beloved animals – but their world is melting away. *Terry Nutkins* on the plight of the polar bear.

Polar bears are one of the most dangerous predators on planet earth. So why do we love them so much? Our fascination goes back a long way. Take Brumas, a polar bear who lived in London Zoo in the 1940s and in nine years attracted three million visitors. He was a celebrity.

I think we are fascinated with them because they remind us of our childhood – those warm and cuddly toy bears that were with us on dark nights when we couldn't sleep. And as humans, we relate to the way mothers interact with their cubs: teaching them, training them, slapping them, cuddling them. I don't have a problem with anthropomorphism: it's how many people learn about, and love, wildlife.

But the polar bears' world is literally melting away.

For many months of the year, while they are mating and looking after their cubs, the bears do not eat. They simply live off the thick layer of fat that lies beneath their double layer of fur, which keeps out the cold of sometimes –40°C or more. It's when this fat layer runs out that the bears are threatened with dying of starvation unless they can find food quickly.

When the ice forms, the polar bears walk out in search of seals. They need to haul them out of their blow holes and on to the floes to eat. Ten years ago I was filming in the Arctic and saw a lone bear walking on the ice. That was the magic of it: one lone bear walking. They are amazing on the ice, when you consider they can weigh 600 kg to 800 kg and are up to two-and-a-half metres tall. Their feet are covered in fur, which helps them move fast and silently, without slipping.

But global warming is taking its toll. Each year, the ice is later in forming. And since no one is giving the polar bears a weather report in their dens, they have to adapt quickly to this late forming of ice. They might have to wait several weeks before they can get on the ice to find prey – and that is the difference between life and death, certainly for the cubs. To allow these bears to survive – and, of course, many other species – we must as a matter of urgency manage our planet.

Guardian

Polar bears: fact file

- Polar bears need sea ice to survive.

- Sea ice is shrinking at a rate of 10% every decade.

- Scientists have found polar bears swimming up to 60 miles in open sea.

- Polar bears are starving, cannibalising each other and coming into human areas to scavenge for food.

- In 30 years the Arctic may have no ice in summer.

- By 2040 there will be a significant decline in the numbers of polar bears.

Your task

Read the newspaper article, 'Take a last look' and the fact file and do the activities below.

1 From paragraph 2, write down two reasons why the writer thinks people love polar bears.

2 Why do you think the writer has chosen to make paragraph 3 only one sentence long?

3 Using your own words, explain two ways in which polar bears are suited to living in the Arctic.

4 a 'So why do we love them so much?' (paragraph 1). What is the effect of the use of 'we' in this question?

   b 'To allow these bears to survive – and, of course, many other species – we must as a matter of urgency manage our planet.' (paragraph 6). What is the effect of this sentence?

5 Write down two examples of geographical language used in this article.

6 Explain how the writer's choice of language suggests that he finds polar bears extraordinary and amazing. In your answer, choose specific words and phrases from the article and comment on them.

7 How does the last paragraph link back to the first?

8 Explain how the layout of this article helps to persuade the reader that people should be concerned about the future of polar bears. In your answer, comment on:

   ● the choice of headline to get the reader's attention
   ● how the picture and the factfile supports the purpose of the article
   ● the way the article is organised and how this helps to persuade the reader.

3 Gothic tales

Objectives

In this unit you will:

Reading
- understand the ways in which texts can reflect literary traditions
- identify and describe the effect of a writers' use of language
- comment on how writers' choices and techniques have an effect on readers.

Composition
- use speech punctuation and commas accurately
- vary sentence length and structure
- use vocabulary precisely.

Conventions
- increase your knowledge of word families.

Speaking and Listening
- present a talk in which the structure and vocabulary make your ideas clear
- have a successful discussion by listening and responding to the ideas of others.

By the end of this unit you will:

- present an audio tour of a haunted house (Speaking and Listening: Speaking and presenting).
- write a horror story (Writing: Composition and conventions)

Cross-curricular links

- **Art and design**
  Cultural understanding and contexts.
- **History**
  Chronological understanding, change and continuity, significance and interpretation.
- **Science**
  Ethical and moral implications.

1 Features of Gothic stories

You are learning:
- to understand the main features of Gothic stories.

Gothic stories became popular around two hundred years ago, and have remained popular ever since. Gothic stories and films are usually about ghosts and horror and they often include these features:
- wild and remote places
- dark and gloomy settings
- graveyards, tombs and corpses
- family curses and dark secrets
- supernatural powers
- mysterious and frightening creatures, people or ghosts
- old, ruined, isolated castles and mansions, often with secret passages and mysterious towers
- nightmares, madness and mental torment
- science used for evil or disastrous purposes
- worrying and unusual natural events (storms, full moons, etc.).

Activity 1

Look carefully at the list of Gothic features above and make a list of stories and films (for example, *Dracula* or *Raven's Gate*) that have some of those features in them.

Activity 2

Read these four story openings:

A Jane leaned on the railing of her apartment balcony, gazed across the shiny, blue sea of the bay, and sighed with happiness. This was going to be the perfect holiday. And best of all, there would be no more Tom.

B Heath Manor finally rose into view behind a line of dense, gloomy fir trees. The closer we got, the more it looked like a brooding monster – battered and bruised, but still menacing. A fierce wind tugged at its broken shutters.

C A sudden dark shadow swept across the bright moon, momentarily blocking out its light. Sarah stumbled against a gravestone that was leaning towards the path like a cracked and crooked tooth. An owl gave a ghostly hoot.

D 'Surrender!' boomed the voice of the Stragor commander. 'Surrender, or we will destroy your ship and all on board.' Martin Strang, leader of Solar Expedition 29, was not easily scared. He readied the stun missile tubes.

Which **two** of these are most Gothic? Briefly explain why.

Activity 3

Frankenstein, by Mary Shelley, is one of the most famous Gothic novels ever written. Read the extract below, which describes the moment when the monster he has been creating finally comes to life.

> How can I describe my emotions at this **catastrophe**, or how **delineate** the wretch whom with such infinite pains and care I had **endeavoured** to form? His limbs were in proportion, and I had selected his features as beautiful. Beautiful! – Great God! His yellow skin scarcely covered the work of muscles and arteries beneath; his hair was of a **lustrous** black, and flowing; his teeth of a pearly whiteness; but these **luxuriances** only formed a more horrid contrast with his watery eyes, that seemed almost of the same colour as the dun white sockets in which they were set, his shrivelled complexion and straight black lips.
>
> The different accidents of life are not so changeable as the feelings of human nature. I had worked hard for nearly two years, for the sole purpose of **infusing** life into an inanimate body. For this I had deprived myself of rest and health. I had desired it with an **ardour** that far exceeded moderation; but now that I had finished, the beauty of the dream vanished, and breathless horror and disgust filled my heart. Unable to endure the **aspect** of the being I had created, I rushed out of the room, and continued a long time **traversing** my bedchamber, unable to compose my mind to sleep.

Biography

Mary Shelley is best known as the author of the novel *Frankenstein*, which was published in 1818. Her husband was the Romantic poet Percy Bysshe Shelley.

Explanations

catastrophe **disaster**
delineate **describe**
endeavoured **tried**
lustrous **shiny**
luxuriances **riches**
infusing **putting**
ardour **passion**
aspect **appearance**
traversing **moving across**

1 Re-write the first sentence of the extract in modern, standard English. How is the language you have used different to Mary Shelley's?

2 Look again at the list of Gothic features on page 58. Write down the ones you find in the extract from *Frankenstein* above.

3 Explain how the narrator feels about the monster he has created. Use a table like the one below to explore his feelings.

Word or phrase	What it might show about the narrator's feelings
catastrophe	Catastrophe means disaster so the narrator feels that he has done a terrible thing.

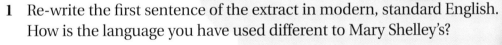

Assess your progress

This table shows you how to get better at the key reading skills used on these two pages. How well are you doing?

	Level 3	Level 4	Level 5
	Pick out and describe some basic features of Gothic texts	Explain how Gothic features are different from those of other sorts of story	Consider how the way a text is written affects its meaning
	Comment on how the reader is supposed to feel	Understand a writer's purpose – even when it is not obvious	Explain the difference between an author's and a character's viewpoints

2 Plot

You are learning:
- to understand how a writer structures a story to try to involve the reader.

Stories are all around us. If we listen to a bit of gossip, watch a soap on TV or read a novel, we are enjoying a story. However, written stories need to be well organised to be really interesting. In other words, they need a **plot**.

Activity 1

Think of a TV programme or a film you saw recently – an episode of *Dr Who*, for example. Write down or tell someone what happened, but just give a **summary**.

A good story is far more than just telling someone what happened. It tries to keep us interested. It starts well and makes us want to continue. The telling of the story has to appeal to our curiosity and sense of excitement.

> **Example:** *Dr Who and his assistant land in London some time in the future and they get taken prisoner by....*

Activity 2

When you have finished your summary of what happened, try writing it so that it works as an interesting story. Write the first few lines.

Look carefully at your two versions of 'what happened'. What changes did you have to make to the summary to make it begin to work as a story that someone would want to read?

> **Example:** *When the Doctor was satisfied that the Tardis had completely settled in its landing-place, he pushed open the door and stepped out into the thick, cold mist beyond. 'Mmmmm!' he moaned in delight. 'Delicious fog. Nothing nicer.'*

Activity 3

The story on page 61 is based on a well-known urban legend. An urban legend is a story that has been told so often and by so many people that it starts to sound like a true story. Often these urban legends have an element of horror.

The writer of this version has tried to put the story into a particular order, to build up the reader's interest. The order of the paragraphs gives the story its plot structure.

The story is only five paragraphs long but the paragraphs have been printed in the wrong order, and the last paragraph has been left out entirely.

1 Put the paragraphs in the best order by writing down their letters: A, B, C and D.

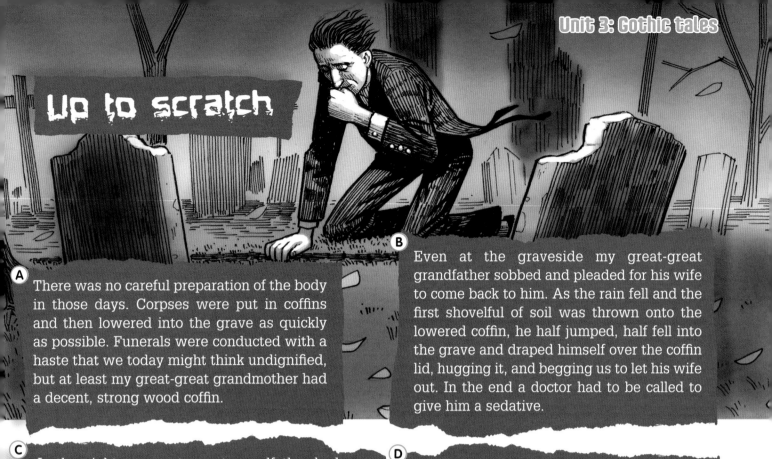

Up to scratch

A There was no careful preparation of the body in those days. Corpses were put in coffins and then lowered into the grave as quickly as possible. Funerals were conducted with a haste that we today might think undignified, but at least my great-great grandmother had a decent, strong wood coffin.

B Even at the graveside my great-great grandfather sobbed and pleaded for his wife to come back to him. As the rain fell and the first shovelful of soil was thrown onto the lowered coffin, he half jumped, half fell into the grave and draped himself over the coffin lid, hugging it, and begging us to let his wife out. In the end a doctor had to be called to give him a sedative.

C In the night my great, great grandfather had a terrible nightmare in which he imagined his wife waking up and desperately trying to claw her way out of the coffin. He screamed and flailed his arms around in his tormented sleep, and when the doctor arrived he begged him to have his wife's coffin dug up. The doctor administered another sedative, but my great-great grandfather was revisited by his nightmare every night that week, and every night he begged the doctor to remove his wife from the grave.

D It is seventy years since my great-great grandmother died. She had been ill for some time and her body had wasted away until she was little more than a scare-crow: tatty, dark clothes draped over a stick-thin frame. Her collar-bones were as fine and fragile as a bird's. But my great-great grandfather was devoted to her until the very end, and when she died he was devastated.

E Missing final paragraph.

2 Write the final paragraph using no more than 100 words.

Sharpen your skills Suffixes

Suffixes are the bits on the ends of words that change or add to those words' meanings. (**Prefixes** do the same job on the *fronts* of words.)

Some common suffixes are: *-ly, -ful, -ible, -able, -tion, -ment, -ic, -al, -ed, -ness*.

1 How many different suffixes can you find in the story 'Up to scratch' above?

2 List as many words as you know that end with the suffix *-ness*.

3 Look carefully at the words in your list. What do you think *-ness* means?

3 Beginnings and endings

You are learning:

● to make the ending of a story relate to its beginning.

Many writers begin their stories in ways that 'hook' the reader.

Activity 1

1 Read the opening of *Night of the Stick Insects* by Alan Durant, below.

You got any pets? Dog, cat, goldfish maybe? Well, Tommy had lots of pets – jars and tanks of them. Tommy bred stick insects, though I guess it wouldn't be quite right to call them 'pets'. His pet was really the gecko lizard that lived in the big glass tank on his chest-of-drawers. Every now and then he'd get that out and, you know, pet it, stroke it, chat to it, that kind of thing. The stick insects, well they had other uses. Some of them, he sold – and he made a fair amount of cash, too. It was amazing how many kids were willing to pay him for the brown stick-like things. At school, there was a craze for them. Tommy thought they were kind of boring himself. They didn't do anything, did they? They just hung about on the wire mesh frame he'd put up against their container wall, imitating twigs. Big deal. He much preferred praying mantises. His dad had a whole collection of those, but he wouldn't let Tommy near them.

2 a How does the writer of *Night of the Stick Insects* try to grab our attention in the opening of the story? He may use a number of ways to do this.

b What do you think will happen in the rest of the story?

Activity 2

1 Now read the end of the story, and see if it helps you to decide what has happened.

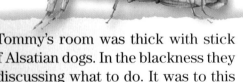

By the dark, dark early hours of the morning, Tommy's room was thick with stick insects, grown to a gigantic size – some the size of Alsatian dogs. In the blackness they hissed and clicked, as if in angry conversation, discussing what to do. It was to this that Tommy awoke …

His first thought was that he was having another nightmare. And even when they lifted him from his bed with their sturdy, tree-trunk limbs, he could not believe it was real, that this was actually happening. It was only when they lifted him towards the huge, open, slimy, tooth-filled mouth of the now monstrous gecko that he understood the full, real horror of the situation. And by then he was half inside and it was too late.

When we watch a film or read a book, we sometimes find that its mood changes. There are many possible moods: happy, tense, jokey, sad, sarcastic, frightening are just some of them.

2 Explain how the mood of the opening is different from the mood of the ending.

You may like to concentrate on comparing the style of the two short extracts here:

> You got any pets? Dog, cat, goldfish maybe? Well, Tommy had lots of pets – jars and tanks of them. (Opening)

3 Often, clues at the beginning of a story help us to *predict* what will happen at the end.

  a Why do you think the stick insects and the gecko became huge?

  b Explain how clues in the opening of the story prepare us for the ending.

> It was only when they lifted him towards the huge, open, slimy, tooth-filled mouth of the now monstrous gecko that he understood the full, real horror of the situation. (Ending)

Activity 3

1 Read the opening of a story called *Home*.

> You know how it is: new houses have new and unfamiliar noises. 'It's to be expected,' Emily's mother reassured her. But that didn't stop Emily waking up with a gasp every night to the ghostly glow of the moon on the revolting zig-zag patterns of the bedroom carpet. And it didn't mean she'd stop worrying about the faint but clear rustling sounds coming from the ancient fireplace – the fireplace that her father had carefully bricked up.

2 What could happen during the story, and how might it end?

3 Write the last 50–100 words of the story.

Assess your progress

Look carefully at the levelled success criteria for features of a good story.

Feature	Level 3	Level 4	Level 5	Level 6
Opening	Express yourself clearly	Choose your style carefully	Use a style that engages the reader	Grab the reader's interest and build their curiosity
Plot development	Don't only put your story in the order in which things happen	Organise ideas well	Explain ideas by developing detail	Structure the story so that each section makes the reader want to read the next one
Ending	Write an interesting ending	Write an ending that 'fits'	Write an engaging ending that 'fits'	Carefully link the ending to the opening

Look at the writing you did for the activities on this page and on page 61.
What will you have to do to move up a level as a story writer?

4 Setting and atmosphere

You are learning:

- how to create an effective setting and atmosphere.

Gothic stories rely heavily on setting and atmosphere. Writers try to create a clear and imaginative setting or 'place' where the action happens. Then they describe that setting in ways that give it a powerful atmosphere or 'mood'.

Activity 1

Think about a scary film or TV programme you have seen. Think about a particularly scary part of it. Make a list of the things that helped to make it so scary. Typical items might include night (setting); creepy music (atmosphere).

Activity 2

In this extract from *The Golem's Eye* by Jonathan Stroud, Kitty is exploring a crypt – a cellar under a church – where people have been buried. She discovers a secret chamber at the end of the crypt. Some words are missing from the extract.

1   Read the extract.

The Secret Chamber

The true end of the chamber was not much further than the illusory one through which she had fallen, perhaps only three metres away from where she stood. The [1] mould had disregarded the false barrier and marched straight through: it clad the walls, and floor, and what lay on the floor, and shone with a [2] radiance in the cold light of her lantern. But despite its thick coating, it did not obscure the objects that lay arranged in a neat row between the walls; their nature was all too clear. There were six of them lying packed together, side by side, their heads flung out towards Kitty, their legs pointing away towards the back wall of the chamber, their [3] hands resting quietly on their chests. The sealed conditions of the crypt had ensured that their flesh had not entirely rotted through; instead it had shrunk about the skeletons, so that the jaws of the skulls were drawn downwards by the [4] skin, giving them permanent expressions of unbridled terror. The skin itself was blackened like fossil wood or tortured leather. The eyes had entirely [5] away. All six were clothed strangely, in old-fashioned suits; heavy boots rested on their lolling feet. The ribcage of one [6] through his shirt. Their hair remained exactly as it had been in life; it flowed from the dreadful heads like [7]. Kitty noticed that one of the men still had a mop of beautiful auburn curls.

2   There are seven gaps in the story. Write the numbers 1 to 7 and next to each number write a good word or phrase to fill the gap in the story. Try to choose words that will build the right atmosphere.

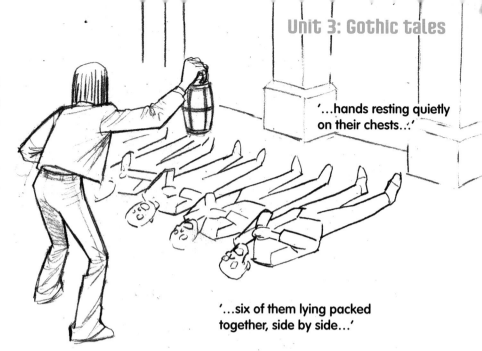

'…hands resting quietly on their chests..'

'…six of them lying packed together, side by side…'

3 Look at this *unfinished* sketch of the scene described in 'The Secret Chamber'. You will also see a couple of quotations linked to details in the sketch. Copy the sketch, finish it, and then add more quotations from the story.

Activity 3

Imagine that you are making a film of 'The Secret Chamber'. How would you create a gripping and creepy atmosphere? Use a storyboard like the one below to develop your ideas in detail.

Shot	Sketch of shot	Camera angle	Lighting	Sound	Music
1					
2					

Sharpen your skills — Adjectives

Sometimes when we write we use dull, unimaginative words such as *nice*, *big*, *dark*, but to create a creepy atmosphere it is important to choose words more carefully.

Imagine you are walking on a quiet country road. You are on your own and lost. You suddenly come across a large, very old, empty-looking house, and you wonder whether to knock and ask for help.

1 Write down at least **ten effective adjectives** to describe the house to make it sound scary. Here are three examples: *gloomy*, *abandoned*, *creaky*. Now think of ten more.

2 When you have done that, try making up **five similes** to describe the house. Here are two examples: *like a blind monster*; *as spooky as a graveyard*. Now think of five more.

You could use a thesaurus and a dictionary to help you find the best words.

5 Character and suspense

You are learning:
- how a writer creates suspense.

There are many ways in which good writers create suspense or 'tension'. They might:
- describe things in ways that worry us
- make us care about characters so that we worry about them
- make a character sound foolishly unaware of what might be about to happen
- make us expect terrible things to happen
- use a variety of sentences to vary the speed of the story (see pages 70–71).

Activity 1

1 Think about the ways in which good writers create suspense as you read this extract from *The Hound of the Baskervilles* by Arthur Conan Doyle. The narrator and Baskerville have very different moods and see things quite differently.

Baskerville Hall

Over the green squares of the fields and the low curve of a wood there rose in the distance a grey, melancholy hill, with a strange jagged summit. Dim and vague in the distance, like some fantastic landscape in a dream. Rolling pasture lands curved upward on either side of us, and old gabled houses peeped out from amid the thick green foliage, but behind the peaceful and sunlit countryside there rose ever, dark against the evening sky, the long, gloomy curve of the moor, broken by the jagged and sinister hills.

At every turn Baskerville gave an exclamation of delight, looking eagerly about him and asking countless questions. To his eyes all seemed beautiful, but to me a tinge of melancholy lay upon the countryside, which bore so clearly the mark of the waning year. Yellow leaves carpeted the lanes and fluttered down upon us as we passed. The rattle of our wheels died away as we drove through drifts of rotting vegetation – sad gifts, as it seemed to me, for Nature to throw before the carriage of the returning heir of the Baskervilles.

Our driver half turned in his seat.

'There's a convict escaped from Princetown, sir. He's been out three days now, and the warders watch every road and every station, but they've had no sight of him yet.'

'Who is he, then?'

'It is Selden, the Notting Hill murderer.'

The road in front of us grew bleaker and wilder, over huge russet and olive slopes, sprinkled with giant boulders. Now and then we passed a moorland cottage, walled and roofed with stone, with no creeper to break its harsh outline. Suddenly we looked down into a cuplike depression, patched with stunted oaks and firs which had been twisted and bent by the fury of years of storm. Two high, narrow towers rose over the trees. The driver pointed with his whip.

Biography

Arthur Conan Doyle (1859–1930)
Arthur Conan Doyle is famous for the many stories he wrote about the detective Sherlock Holmes, who never failed to solve a crime, however complicated. Conan Doyle also wrote adventure stories, featuring a character called Professor Challenger.

'Baskerville Hall,' said he.

Its master had risen and was staring with flushed cheeks and shining eyes. The lodge was a ruin of black granite and bared ribs of rafters.

Through the gateway we passed into the avenue, where the wheels were again hushed amid the leaves, and the old trees shot their branches in a sombre tunnel over our heads. Baskerville shuddered as he looked up the long, dark drive to where the house glimmered like a ghost at the farther end.

2   Using a table like the one below, list all the words and phrases that create a happy, calm atmosphere and all the words and phrases that create a tense, worried atmosphere.

Happy and calm	Tense and worrying
Rolling pasture	Jagged summit

3   Look again at the list of ways writers can create suspense or tension on page 66.

   a   Explain how some of these ways are used in the extract above to create suspense. How does the writer make us feel that things are going to turn out badly?
   b   How do Baskerville's feelings change during the extract?

Assess your progress

The table below shows you how to improve your story-writing.

Level 3	Level 4	Level 5	Level 6
• Use some adjectives • Create exciting moments	• Use descriptions • Deliberately use some ways of building tension	• Use different ways to add interest, including dialogue • Deliberately try to engage the reader	• Express and describe feelings and moods in detail • Deliberately use Gothic conventions

Here is a student's own continuation of the Baskerville Hall passage. What level does it fit? How do you know?

'It's not how I remember it,' said Baskerville, looking worried.

We got closer to the house. We could see its dark and dirty

windows. Why didn't someone clean them and let the light in?

The carriage wheels crunched on the driveway.

6 Dialogue

You are learning:
- how dialogue can make a story more vivid.

Dialogue is the word for people talking to each other in a story or in a play. When characters talk to each other in a soap opera such as *Neighbours* or *Coronation Street,* they are using dialogue. If writers simply described things and summarised for us what characters say, their stories would seem flat and dull. We want to 'hear' the characters speak. The *way* they speak makes them sound real and believable.

Activity 1

Here is a piece of 'reported speech':

> John apologised to Sarah for not being able to go to the cinema on Saturday because he was going shopping with his mother to get some new shoes. Sarah was disappointed and annoyed because he had promised he was coming and she'd already bought the tickets.

Now turn it into a piece of dialogue, beginning:
'I'm really sorry,' said John, 'but …'

Activity 2

1 You see dialogue in play scripts as well as in stories. Read this play script:

The Short Way Home

Tom and Emma are walking together

Tom: Come on, hurry up. I'm going to be in so much trouble if I'm late home again. It's alright for you – your parents never seem to notice if you're out or in.

Emma: Oh stop flapping. We'll get there. Anyway, we only have to cut across the cemetery and slip through the gap in the hedge and we'll be there in half the time.

Tom: You have got to be joking. I'm not going through the cemetery in the dark. It's too spooky. Jo Penny down our street took a short cut through there and was never seen again.

Emma: Don't be silly. No one knows how Jo Penny disappeared, and no one knows where either. Just because they found her scarf in the cemetery doesn't mean she was ever there.

Tom: Well you'll never find ME there anyway.

They reach the cemetery. They stop.

Emma: And you'll never find me either. Good night, scaredy!

Emma turns and runs into the cemetery.

Tom: You idiot, Emma. Come back. I'm not chasing you, and I'm not waiting for you either. Emma! *(Pause)* I don't like this, Emma. *(Pause)* I'm going.

Emma: *(Calling from some way off)* Come and get me – if you dare.

2 What are the differences between Emma and Tom's personalities? How does the way they speak show their personalities?

3 Rewrite 'The Short Way Home' as a story instead of a script. (Tip: look below at the rules for speech punctuation.) Start your story like this:

Sarah and Tom walked together down the dark street, Tom slightly ahead.

'Come on, hurry up!' Tom pleaded with Sarah, 'I'm going to be in so much trouble if I'm late home again. It's alright for you – your parents never seem to notice if you're out or in.'

Sharpen your skills Speech punctuation

There are three rules for speech punctuation:

- Put speech marks at the beginning and end of the words that a character actually speaks.

- Begin the speech with a capital letter and put a punctuation mark inside the end speech marks: a full stop (.), a comma (,), an exclamation mark (!) or a question mark (?).

- Start a new paragraph whenever you change speaker.

Here is some dialogue from a story:

I can't see you called Tom Are you over by the gate No Sarah replied I'm nearly through the gap in the hedge Where are you

Write out these lines, putting in the correct punctuation and paragraphing.

7 Narrative devices

You are learning:

- to use a range of narrative devices to involve the reader, and to recognise how writers convey setting, character and mood through word choice and sentence structure.

Writers only have words to grab and hold a reader's attention, so it is essential that they choose their words very carefully and design their sentences for maximum effect.

Activity 1

In the following extract from *Raven's Gate* by Anthony Horowitz, Matt is being chased by some ghastly dogs. The writer is trying to create excitement and tension.

1   Read the extract.

Hideous dogs

The first of the creatures had already halved the distance between itself and Matt, yet it didn't seem to be moving fast. It hovered in the air between each bound, barely touching the grass before jumping up again. There was something hideous about the way it ran. A panther or leopard closing in for the kill has a certain majesty. But the dog was deformed, lopsided, ghastly. The flesh on one of its flanks had rotted and a glistening ribcage jutted out. As if to avoid the stench of the wound, the animal had turned away, its head hanging close to its front paws. Strings of saliva trailed from its mouth. And every time its feet hit the ground, its whole body quivered, threatening to collapse in on itself.

Matt reached the fence and clawed at it with his hands, crashing his fingers against the wire. He thought he had run in a straight line, following the way he had come, but he seemed to have got it wrong. He couldn't find the gap. He looked behind him. Two more bounds and the dogs would reach him. There was no doubt that they would tear him apart. He could almost feel their teeth tearing into him, ripping the flesh away from his bones. He had never seen anything so ferocious … not in a zoo, not in a film, not anywhere in the real world.

2   Anthony Horowitz uses a number of techniques to create excitement and tension. Copy and complete this table, then explain at least two other ways he does this.

Way of creating tension and excitement	Example	How it works in the extract
Using vivid, unusual words that feed our imaginations	ghastly	This sounds a bit like 'ghostly' so it is frightening straight away. Also 'ghastly' sounds unhealthy and rather disgusting.
Repeating words and phrases to build up a fast rhythm		
Using short sentences for impact		

Writers often end chapters with something that arouses our curiosity and makes us want to read on. This sort of chapter ending is called a **cliff hanger**.

Activity 2

1 Read this extract from near the end of the 'Hideous Dogs' chapter of *Raven's Gate*.

2 Below are three possible endings for the chapter. One of them is the ending that Anthony Horowitz actually used. Which version makes the best cliff hanger?

Matt felt a thump as they drove over the body of one of the dying creatures. But where was the other? He looked around, then yelled out as, still blazing, it slammed into the windscreen, launching itself out of nowhere. For a few seconds it was in front of him, its dreadful teeth centimetres from his face. Then Richard changed into first gear and wrenched the wheel. The dog spun away. Matt looked out of the back window. The flickering remains of one carcass lay in the middle of the road. The second had got snarled up in the wheels, but as the car sped forward it fell free and was tossed to one side.

A

They accelerated away, not looking back again. They got home by midnight, and at last they felt safe.

B

Richard pulled a face and opened the window. 'So, do you mind telling me what that was all about?' he demanded. Matt didn't know where to begin. 'I think something is happening in Lesser Malling,' he said. Richard nodded. 'I think you could be right.'

C

'Take that!' Richard yelled as he accelerated off the track and onto the firm road. The car swerved a couple of times before settling down and hurtling into darkness. They didn't speak all the way home. When they got there they parked carefully on the drive and went to bed.

Sharpen your skills — Simple, complex and compound sentences

Here is some very dull writing. Each sentence is a simple sentence. How could you vary the sentences to make them more interesting to read?

There was moonlight. The curtains were open. I saw a woman. She was lying still on the bed in a white robe. A demon was sitting on her. I was scared.

Rewrite these lines to make them exciting and full of tension. Don't invent any new details; just improve the words and the style.

8 Developing character

You are learning:
- to appreciate how a writer creates expectations in a reader and gets them interested in characters.

On page 58 you learnt about the typical features of Gothic stories. When we come across these features in a story, we expect that it will involve ghosts or horror.

Activity 1

1 Read the opening of *Coraline* by Neil Gaiman.

> Coraline discovered the door a little while after they moved into the house.
>
> It was a very old house – it had an attic under the roof and a cellar under the ground and an overgrown garden with huge old trees in it.
>
> Coraline's family didn't own all of the house; it was too big for that. Instead they owned part of it.
>
> There were other people who lived in the old house.

2 Make a list of the words or phrases that suggest *Coraline* is going to be a ghost or horror story. Explain each of your choices in a table like the one here.

Word	Explanation
door	Coraline *discovers* the door and this suggests it is hidden and secret. So it is mysterious and could lead somewhere scary.

Activity 2

If we get interested in characters then we start to care about them, and the writer can make us worry about what is going to happen to them.

1 Read how the opening of *Coraline* continues:

Miss Spink and Miss Forcible lived in the flat below Coraline's, on the ground floor. They were both old and round, and they lived in their flat with a number of ageing Highland terriers who had names like Hamish and Andrew and Jock. Once upon a time Miss Spink and Miss Forcible had been actresses, as Miss Spink told Coraline the first time she met her.

'You see, Caroline,' Miss Spink said, getting Coraline's name wrong, 'both myself and Miss Forcible were famous actresses in our time. We trod the boards, lovey. Oh, don't let Hamish eat the fruit-cake, or he'll be up all night with his tummy.'

'It's Coraline. Not Caroline. Coraline,' said Coraline.

2 We know that Miss Spink and Miss Forcible used to be actresses, but what can we work out about them as people? In other words, what are they *like*?

Here are some words that might be used to describe the two old ladies.

stupid   lovely   cruel   **creepy**   bossy
kind   amusing   odd   boastful   disgusting

a Which **two** words in the list **best** describe the old ladies?
b Explain why you have chosen each of those words.
c Which word is **least** true of the old ladies? Why?
d Use two of **your own words** to describe what the old ladies are like.
e How might the story continue? Try to write the next five lines.

Activity 3

1 Read how Neil Gaiman introduces another character.

In the flat above Coraline's, under the roof, was a crazy old man with a big moustache. He told Coraline that he was training a mouse circus. He wouldn't let anyone see it.

'One day, little Caroline, when they are all ready, everyone in the whole world will see the wonders of my mouse circus. You ask me why you cannot see it now. Is that what you asked me?'

'No,' said Coraline quietly. 'I asked you not to call me Caroline. It's Coraline.'

2 a What do you think the old man is like? Why?
b What do you think Coraline is like? Why?

Sharpen your skills — Commas

Commas have many uses. These include:
- ending a subordinate clause at the start of a sentence
- providing a dramatic pause.
- adding extra information to sentences
- separating items in a list

Look at the commas that Neil Gaiman uses in *Coraline*. Choose three commas and try to explain what each one is doing. Try to choose commas that do different things.

9 Attention to detail

You are learning:
- to involve a reader by using a lot of imaginative detail.

Good stories usually have a lot of rich detail that stirs up the reader's imagination, allowing them to 'see' a scene in their head.

Activity 1

Many of the early Gothic writers were fascinated and inspired by Henry Fuseli's 1781 painting *The Nightmare*. Look carefully at the painting. What do you see?

1 Write down everything that you see. Try to be very factual, for example, 'The woman's left arm is dangling over the bed with the knuckles just touching the floor.'

2 Now write down possible explanations for what you see. For example, 'The woman might be limp because she is dead, deeply asleep or drugged.'

Assess your progress

You have tried to notice all the detail in the painting and make sense of it. Some students were asked to 'write the painting' as though it was a scene from a story. Here are the criteria the students used to help them improve their writing:

Level 3	Level 4	Level 5	Level 6
• Use some adjectives to add interest • Try to entertain your reader and use the same narrator throughout • Use at least three Gothic features • Write clear, simple sentences, begun with capital letters and ended with full stops	• Use adverbs and adjectives to add detail • Establish a clear viewpoint (e.g. a narrator) and sense of purpose in your story • Use Gothic features • Control sentences	• Develop details using similes or metaphors • Maintain a viewpoint and clear sense of purpose throughout the writing • Use unusual ways of interesting the reader • Maintain a Gothic 'flavour' • Vary sentences for effect	• Use some original and very engaging ideas • Express and explain opinions, attitudes or feelings in detail • Adopt an original viewpoint • 'Grip' the reader • Vary the Gothic form to be original • Use varied and complex sentences, sometimes starting with subordinate clauses

Here is part of one student's version of the painting-as-a-story.
This version is good enough for a Level 5.

> As I entered the room the moon came out from behind the clouds and flooded the room with a pale, white light. Sarah was lying on the table. She was stretched out, wearing a long, white robe. My heart thumped because she looked dead. Her head was hanging over the edge of the table and one arm was dangling.

Look back at the criteria. What level would you give to this second version? Why?

> I knew I was too late. In the moonlight coming from the open window, Jane was draped over the bed in the centre of the room. Robed in a beautiful white gown, her head and arm hung peacefully over the table's edge, but blood had soaked into her outer robe. Her face and neck had a corpse-like paleness. On her body sat a mean and triumphant demon, his grinning shadow printed grimly on the red curtains behind.

Now try writing your own version of the painting. Make sure you use the criteria to guide you in making your writing as good as possible.

10 Language for effect

Writers – and speakers – always have to choose their words carefully. This is true of non-fiction as well as stories. Being careful means thinking hard about:

● *what* you are trying to achieve
● *who* your audience (or reader) is.

For instance, if you want to give *information* to a group of ten-year-olds, you would choose simple, straightforward language and you could use some slang words. On the other hand, if you wanted to *persuade* your headteacher to reduce your homework, you would have to choose words and a style that were much more formal.

Activity 1

A tourist attraction called Nightmare Alleys has recently opened in London. Visitors explore life-size models of old buildings and streets where terrible crimes and accidents have taken place, and which are widely believed to be haunted.

1 Read this leaflet, designed to persuade people to visit Nightmare Alleys.

Nightmare Alleys

Dusk gropes its way stealthily through the tightly-packed alleyways and courtyards of old London, filling its inhabitants with dread and scattering them to seek shelter in their cramped and poorly-lit homes. As darkness tightens its grip on the city's slums, spooky shadows slip around corners and lie in wait for their prey. The city's deathly secrets, so long shut up in these grimy walls, are stirring and returning to haunt their old hideouts: the silhouette of a well-dressed gentleman sharpens his knife and blends patiently into a broken doorway. Sinister and cruel threats whisper around the courtyard walls. A sudden scream pierces the eerie quiet.

The only people who dare remain in these grim alleyways are the insane, the foolish, the homeless – and you.

London's newest and spookiest attraction is open for business. Come and explore the Nightmare Alleys of old London. Thrill to the authentic sounds, sights and smells of the city's close-packed slums. Be haunted by the ghosts of notorious killers such as Jack the Ripper and Sweeney Todd, and their unfortunate victims. Feel the hairs rise on your neck as you step across the mass graves of the plague dead.

You never know what is waiting for you round the next corner.
Come and find out – if you dare!

2   The writer uses a number of ways to persuade us to visit Nightmare Alleys. For example, she uses the present tense to make us feel like we are already there, and she uses unusual and threatening words.

   a   Find and write down an example of:
   - the present tense
   - threatening words.
   b   Write down and explain at least two other ways the writer uses to make us want to visit Nightmare Alleys.

Activity 2

The owners of Nightmare Alleys decided to publicise the attraction in a number of ways in order to appeal to different types of people. Here is part of a radio advert aimed at London teenagers.

Radio advert script

Sound of creaking door echoing.

Emily	Oooooh, I don't like it – it's spooky in 'ere.
Tim	You go first. I can't see a flippin' thing.
Emily	Come on then, but 'old me 'and.

Spooky music, building up. Shuffling footsteps. Whispering voices. Sudden silence.

Emily	Tim? What's up? Oooh, yer 'and's all dry and rough. Tim? *She screams suddenly*
Voice over	Nightmare Alleys. London's newest and spookiest attraction. Just five minutes from The London Dungeon. But years back in time. It's *so* not boring.
Emily	(*Nervously*) Tim? I know I've got yer 'and, but shouldn't there be a you on the end of it?
Voice over	Nightmare Alleys. Open all year round. ...[*slogan missed out*]

1   Explain how this advert tries to appeal to young people.

2   The final slogan has been missed out of the script. Here are three possible slogans:
   a Visit us soon
   b Your worst nightmare … and some
   c It's spooky
   Which is the best slogan, and which is the worst? Why?

3   Think up a better slogan of your own. Explain why it is a good slogan.

4   If possible, work with a group of students to act out and record the Nightmare Alleys radio advert, finishing with the best slogan.

Assessment task

Speaking and Listening: Speaking and presenting

Welcome to Murder Manor!

You are now going to prepare a Speaking and Listening task in a group. This is one of your main assessments in this Gothic unit.

Your task

You are the publicity team for Murder Manor, an Elizabethan house that is open to the public. You have been asked to prepare a commentary about the Manor for visitors to listen to on headphones.

Preparing for your Speaking and Listening assessment task

There are two parts to this assessment:
- Group planning
- Group presentation

You need to make sure you get along with the other members of your group and that you help each other to work successfully.

1 Look carefully at the layout of Murder Manor and agree the best route through the building.

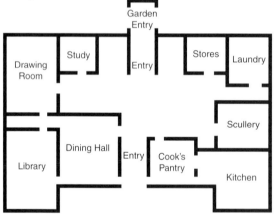

2 Agree a role for each member of your group.

Chairperson:
You are responsible for leading the discussion. You must make sure everyone has their say and the task gets done.

Scribe:
You are responsible for making a note of every decision that is taken by the group.

Other members of the group:
You are responsible for taking an active part in the discussion, listening to others and following the instructions of the Chairperson.

3 Look together at the success criteria for group planning and the presentation:

	Level 3	Level 4	Level 5	How to do it
Group planning	• Listen. • Reply to others. • Show you are thinking about what other people say.	• Listen carefully. • Contribute ideas. • Ask questions about other people's ideas and views.	• Pay close attention to what others say. • Make contributions that take account of others' views. • Ask questions to develop ideas.	• Make notes; nod; say things like 'OK', 'I see'. • Only speak when you have something good to say. Make your views clear. • Be polite. Be patient. Show respect for other people's ideas and feelings.
Presentation	• Attempt to adapt a more formal style. • Use some simple signposts to guide your listeners. • Express yourself using some of the right words. • Try to order your commentary.	• Use some formal standard English words and grammar. • Try to make your language appropriate for your listeners. • Express yourself simply and clearly, using the right words. • Put your commentary into a useful order.	• Use mostly formal, standard English. • Try to capture your listeners' interest. • Use the right words and style. • Make sure your commentary is well organised.	• Plan. • Think carefully about the words you use: are they right for the listener? Will they have the effect you want them to have? Are they interesting? • Speak clearly and vary your tone. • Try to sound lively.

4 a As a group, plan your commentary recording so that your discussions and the commentary will meet at least the Level 5 criteria.

 b Discuss in detail how you will have to talk, listen and behave to meet those criteria. Use the 'How to do it' column above as a starting point for your discussion.

 c Keep referring back to the criteria as you work together, and talk about the progress you are making.

5 Decide which rooms or parts of the Manor House your group is going to cover (your group could include some of its own ideas here).

6 a Decide what you are going to say about each room or part of the house.

 b Agree who is going to present the commentary for each room or part of the house. Each person should then make some notes about what they are going to say (remember you should not write out every word).

8 Practise giving your commentary for each room in turn, remembering the success criteria above.

11 Planning a story

You are learning:
- to organise and develop a story.

It's almost impossible to write out a story that's perfect first time; the best stories are planned and developed in meticulous detail.

Activity 1

Here is a 'story':

The Curse

She was digging in the garden when she found a little old box. She thought it was a bit funny. She took it to her dad. He opened it and an ancient curse got out and started killing people. She chased the curse round an old ruined castle. In the end she managed to defeat the curse and she was a hero.

What is wrong with this 'story'? Why doesn't it work? How could it be improved? Use a table like the one below to note down your ideas.

What is wrong with the story	How it could be improved

A good story is not just a list of things that happen; it needs to be organised and developed. In other words, it needs to have a **structure**. Many stories follow something like the structure shown in the diagram below.

1. **Setting the scene and characters** — Background to places, characters and what happened before the story started. This helps to draw the reader in. Some stories start with action and then pause to set the scene.

2. **Problem** — The main character meets a challenge or a problem. Their normal life is disturbed. Something unusual and startling happens.

3. **Adjustment** — The character gets used to the problem so that it no longer troubles them. However, they might have been changed in some way. Through this we learn things about the character and perhaps they learn about themselves.

4. Complication   This is a new, larger and trickier problem for the main character. They probably have to make a difficult decision that tests their strength of character.

5. Adjustment   Again the character comes to terms with this new, larger problem. They are probably left changed in some important way.

6. Crisis   Because the main character never completely solved the problem or complication, a much larger problem – a crisis – happens. They can't just cope with this crisis; they have to do something dramatic and life-changing.

7. Resolution   Lessons are learnt by the character or the reader – or both. Problems are sorted out – perhaps forever, perhaps just for the time being.

Activity 2

Here is the opening of 'The Curse' rewritten to fit the first step in our suggested story structure:

1 Look back at the advice given for the first step in the suggested story structure. How is the rewritten opening of 'The Curse' better than the first version?

2 What can we work out about Sam and about what happened before the story started?

3 Look back at the original version of 'The Curse'. What could happen at each of the other six steps in the suggested story structure? Don't write the story; just make notes for each step in the structure.

It was while Sam was digging in her father's vegetable patch that she found the box. She was angrily thrusting the spade deep into his prize onions, chopping through the leaves and bulbs, when the spade hit something hard and unyielding.

'Oww!' she had yelled, throwing the spade to one side and shaking her jarred hand in pain and fury. It really wasn't fair that taking justified revenge on her father should cause her further harm.

Activity 3

Of course, a very long story may have a far longer sequence of crises and adjustments than the sequence in our story structure.

1 How many of the steps in our story structure would you expect to see in the first chapter of a novel?

2 Which step would you expect the first chapter to end with?

Assess your progress

1 Look back through everything you have done in this section. Make a list of the most important things you have learnt about writing stories.

2 Write down three things that you will you need to do to make the next story you write the best one you have ever written. Make sure you look at the improvement criteria on page 75.

Assessment task

Writing: Composition and conventions

The Castle with a Secret

You are a successful writer of horror stories. You are about to write the opening chapter of your next book, which is set in a huge, half-ruined castle.

Your task

Write the opening chapter of a horror story, ending with a cliff hanger, so that the reader will want to read on. You should include:

- some features of horror stories
- carefully chosen words and phrases to build up a spooky, scary atmosphere
- a variety of sentence types and a range of punctuation.

You could begin your first chapter:

As I came out of the woods, I could see the towers of the castle against the blood red of the sunset ...

Story checklist

Use the list below to check that you have included some of the relevant features that your story is going to be assessed on.

Features	✓ I have included this
Carefully chosen words and phrases to create a: • spooky setting • mysterious character • sense of tension.	
A variety of sentences: • simple sentences • compound sentences • complex sentences.	
A range of punctuation: • capital letters and full stops • commas • punctuation of speech.	

Remember to check your work carefully before you hand it in!

4 Our world

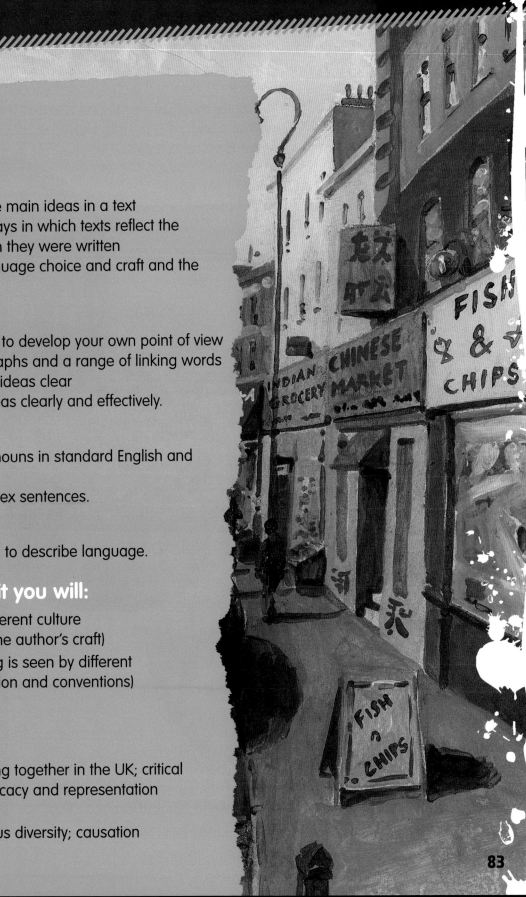

Objectives

In this unit you will:

Reading
- identify and understand the main ideas in a text
- understand the different ways in which texts reflect the society and culture in which they were written
- comment on a writer's language choice and craft and the effect this has on readers.

Composition
- use evidence and opinions to develop your own point of view
- use well-structured paragraphs and a range of linking words and phrases to make your ideas clear
- organise a text to show ideas clearly and effectively.

Conventions
- understand the use of pronouns in standard English and use them in your writing
- understand and use complex sentences.

Language
- understand the terms used to describe language.

By the end of this unit you will:

- read something from a different culture
  (Reading: Understanding the author's craft)
- write about how something is seen by different cultures (Writing: Composition and conventions)

Cross-curricular links

- **Citizenship**
  Identities and diversity; living together in the UK; critical thinking and enquiry; advocacy and representation
- **History**
  Cultural, ethnic and religious diversity; causation

1 Features of texts from different cultures

You are learning:
- to recognise some key features of texts from different cultures.

Culture influences how stories are told. Cultural influences may be seen in what the story is about, the story's narrative structure or the language of the characters' speech. The writer may use words and phrases that are not standard English to show the speech patterns of the culture.

Explanations

Standard English is spoken and written language that is thought to be clear and correct. In writing, standard English is correct in both its spelling and grammar. It is the English you are expected to use in school.

Activity 1

1   What are the cultural traditions of the country you live in? Think about the areas listed below; the first one is done for you.

- Popular food: fish and chips, chicken tikka masala, burgers, sausage and mash, pizza.
- Leisure activities
- Holidays and celebrations
- Music
- Dress.

2   Do you think any of these traditions have come from other countries?

3   Is your life different from the lives of people in other countries? How?

Biography

Grace Nichols (1950–)
Grace Nichols is an award-winning poet born in Georgetown, Guyana in 1950. After working in Guyana as a teacher and journalist, she emigrated to the UK in 1977. A lot of her poetry features Caribbean rhythms and culture.

Activity 2

1   Read the poem by Grace Nichols about a childhood experience in church in Guyana in South America.

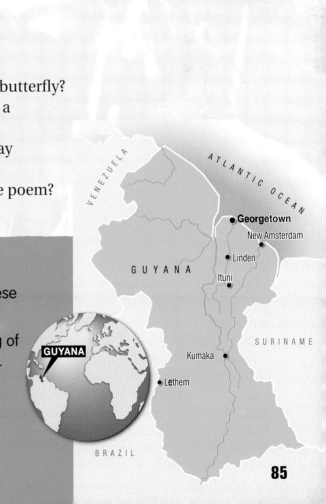

Be a Butterfly
Don't be a kyatta-pilla
Be a butterfly
old preacher screamed
to illustrate his sermon
5 of Jesus and the higher life
rivulets of well-earned
sweat sliding down
his muscly mahogany face
in the half-empty school church
10 we sat shaking with muffling
laughter
watching our mother trying to save
herself from joining the wave
only our father remaining poker face
15 and afterwards we always went home to
split peas Sunday soup
with dumplings, fufu and pigtail

Don't be a kyatta-pilla
Be a butterfly
20 Be a butterfly

That was de life preacher
and you was right

2 a What is the connection between a caterpillar and a butterfly?
b What do you think the preacher means by 'Don't be a caterpillar, be a butterfly'?
c Find examples of words or phrases that show the way English is spoken in Guyana.
d What do you learn about Guyanese culture from the poem?

Assess your progress

1 List three similarities and three differences between Guyanese culture and your own culture.

2 Complete the sentences below to show your understanding of the skills needed when reading texts from different cultures.

Texts from different cultures often show similarities between different cultures and our own. For example...
They also show some differences. These might include...

85

2 Identifying main ideas

You are learning:
● to select relevant evidence from a text.

When you write about a story, you need evidence to support your ideas and opinions. You can use phrases or sentences from the text to do this.

Activity 1

1 *Refugee Boy* tells the story of Alem, whose family are caught up in the war between Ethiopia and Eritrea. His father sends him to England to escape the war. The story describes Alem's experience of two cultures: his home in Africa and as a refugee in England. Read this extract from *Refugee Boy* by Benjamin Zephaniah.

Chapter 3   This is War

My name is Alem Kelo. My age is fourteen. I am from Africa. I was born in an area called Badme. Some people think this area is a part of Eritrea and some people think that this area is part of Ethiopia. My father taught me that it was a part of Africa and he said that there is no country in Africa that is bigger than Africa. In 1991 when the big war was over, I was five years old. My father and my mother went to live in Asmara.

My father can speak six languages – Arabic, Afar, Tigrinya, Italian, English and Amharic. My mother can also speak these languages but I can only speak Amharic, Tigrinya and English. But I want to learn many more languages and I want to make my English better. When I was ten years old we all went to live in Harar. Harar is in Ethiopia, high in the hills, the sun shines bright there but it is very cool. I found a new school and I had a good friend there, his name is Dawit. My mother found a new job in the bank and my father was the manager of the biggest post office in the city.

We were happy living there until war broke out again and we began to have problems. Some of the other children at school started to pick on me, not Dawit but some others, and then one day my mother came home and said that she had lost her job because nobody did want to work with her. She said the manager said she was causing too much trouble, the Ethiopian workers said that they were at war with Eritrea, so they will not work with someone from Eritrea. She was very upset. And then some weeks later my father said the people at work said that he must leave my mother because she is Eritrean and she is the enemy. My father said no, and he kept on working there but I think it was difficult for him. Sometimes he came home from work and he didn't talk to us and I think this was because he was having problems at work. And then one night when we were asleep, the police broke down the door of our house and then they began to break up the house. My father told them that he was born in Ethiopia, so they said that if he loves Ethiopia he can stay but me and my mother must go.

Then one day – it was my birthday – my father said I should have a holiday. He said that a holiday would make me happy and I would forget the problems. My mother was trying to find a job, she said she would not come, so my father took me to Djibouti by bus and from there we flew to Addis Ababa and from there we flew to England. I was thinking that we came here for a holiday, so that I could practise my English and see the buildings, but my father left me here so that I will not die.

2 Use a timeline like the one on the right to show where Alem was living and what happened there.

3 Alem's father is from Ethiopia. His mother is from Eritrea. Why do some people in the story think that this is a problem?

4 Identify three things that happened to Alem's family because of the war starting.

Born   Age 5   Age 10   Age 14

Activity 2

1 Which of the statements below do you agree with and which do you disagree with?

2 Find quotations to support each of the statements you agree with. The first example is done for you.

		Agree/Disagree	Quotation
1	Alem's family are intelligent and educated.	Agree	'My father can speak six languages... My mother can also speak these languages.'
2	Alem's father is willing to stand up for his beliefs.		
3	Alem's father deceives Alem.		
4	Alem's father deceives his mother.		

Sharpen your skills Parts of a sentence

subject   verb   object

The brothers ate their dinner.

Explanations

> subject tells us who or what a sentence is about
> verb tells us what a person or thing does
> object tells us who or what has been affected by the action of the verb

1 Write out the sentences below, then circle the verbs and underline and label the subject and object.
- Some of the children at the school picked on Alem.
- The police frightened Alem's family.

2 Write out two simple sentences with Alem as the subject of the sentence and another family member as the object. Underline and label the subject and object.

3 Narrative point of view

You are learning:
- to understand the difference between first- and third-person narrative and why authors choose a narrative point of view.

Writers make choices about who tells a story.

We ate our dinner in silence.
First-person narrative A character who is part of the story uses *I* and *we* to tell the story. This allows the reader to see what the character is thinking and feeling from their perspective.

They ate their dinner in silence.
Third-person narrative The story is told by someone outside the story using *he, she* and *they*.

Activity 1

Look at the extract from *Refugee Boy* on pages 86–7 and answer these questions.

1 Does Zephaniah use the first-person or the third-person narrative? Find a line from the extract to support your answer.

2 Why do you think Zephaniah chose this narrative point of view?

3 How does Zephaniah suggest that English is not Alem's first language?

4 Alem's culture and experiences may be different from your own. Can you see any similarities between him and yourself?

Activity 2

1 Read the passage from Chapter 4 of *Refugee Boy*. Alem is being interviewed by two women from the Refugee Council in Britain.

When the tea making was done, Mariam began talking as Pamela made notes.

'Right, Alem, as we said earlier, this organisation is called the Refugee Council. We are independent and our main concern is to look after the interests of refugees. Unfortunately it's not up to us whether you can stay in Britain but we will try our best to make sure that the Home Office knows why you should stay.'

Once again Alem looked puzzled. 'I don't want to stay,' he said. 'I don't really want to stay here, I want to go home – to Africa.'

Mariam responded quickly. 'But you know why your father and mother had to get you out, don't you?'

'Of course I do, I told you why, but I don't want to stay here for ever. It's cold.'

Mariam smiled. 'Yes, we know it's cold and we hope that you don't have to stay here for ever, but do you really want to go home right now? Do you think it's safe?'

There was a long silence before Alem replied. He took time to think through his answer and as he answered he placed every word carefully. 'I want to go home but I can't go now because of the fighting. So I would like to go home when there is peace. Most of all I want to be with my parents.'

2 Now answer the following questions:

a Why does Alem not want to stay in Britain? What does this show about Alem's understanding of his situation?

b Do you think Mariam wants to help Alem? How can you tell?

c Does Zephaniah use a first- or third-person narrator in this passage? Why do you think Zephaniah chose this narrative point of view?

d From the extract, choose three sentences where Mariam and Alem talk to each other. Rewrite these sentences from Alem's point of view, including his thoughts and feelings. Does what you have written change your attitude to Mariam?

Sharpen your skills — Auxiliary verbs

Auxiliary verbs help to explain the main verb in a verb phrase.

auxiliary verbs
Mariam <u>had</u> <u>been</u> making the tea.

Write the text for three questions that Alem might want to ask on his arrival in England. Use an auxiliary verb in each one and underline it. An example has been done for you.

'Where <u>will</u> I live?'

Assess your progress

Choose a traffic light to show how confident you are at recognising and writing in the first person.

not confident

quite confident

very confident

4 Setting and character

You are learning:
- to understand how writers use language to describe setting and character.

When we read stories, we often see the characters and settings in our minds. Writers make this happen through their choice of language: every word is chosen carefully for its effect on the reader.

Activity 1

1 Read the extract below from a novel by Andrée Chedid. Sybil, a young American girl, is visiting Beirut, the capital of Lebanon, with her grandmother. Civil war is about to break out.

The Story of Sybil

In Odette's district, the bazaar with the scarlet shop front was the first to be blown to pieces. The store was to the left of the square. Sybil often went there. From when she was small, she had been used to doing the shopping, and Odette and Kalya had just given her permission to run a few errands instead of Slimane.

The shopkeeper, Aziz, was a man loved by all, with his chubby face and round eyes. Several times a day, he would stop what he was doing as soon as he heard the muezzin's call, and pray. He wore a brown skullcap on his bald head and took great care of the thick moustache that drooped on either side of his mouth.

Aziz took pride in proving to his new customers – the old ones were already convinced – that you could find anything and everything in his booth! The little girl had great fun asking him for some unusual item, just to see if he had it: a yo-yo, a scoobeedoo, a Beatles record or a carnival mask. In less than a minute, he would pull the object out from an indescribable jumble of things and hold it up triumphantly.

'Stamps, newspapers, magazines – in three languages – toothpaste, chewing-gum, polishes, beer, paper handkerchiefs, cigarettes, beauty creams, whisky and tambourines, needles, balls of wool, toys, balloons, aspirin... You can ask for anything you want, since I've got it all!'

This list filled him with joy, and he could have gone on for hours, punctuating it with the word 'since'. 'Since' constantly recurred in his speech, as if a relation between cause and effect gave his existence coherence and linked together the numerous and assorted objects that filled his tiny shop.

The shopkeeper pulled at the huge drawer of a dilapidated chest but it was jammed. His arms taut, he pulled again. There were beads of sweat on his brow and on the fuzzy black hair that his unbuttoned, brightly coloured shirt revealed.

'Drawer of the devil, open, since I command you to do so!' It gave way so suddenly that he fell over backwards, waving his arms and legs in the air. Sybil could barely suppress her laughter.

'Laugh! Don't be ashamed to laugh since it's funny and since I haven't broken any bones!'

He laughed at it too. She helped him up. He finally took a little inlaid box out of the drawer, which was crammed full of cheap knick-knacks. He lifted the lid and it played a shrill tune to which Aziz hummed dreamily.

'It's a song from Paris.'

'Have you been to Paris?'

'One day, I'll travel too! On the day Paris was liberated, the crowd sang and clapped. Here in this square. You weren't born then. Do me a favour, take this box, it's for you. For your grandmother, take this bunch of grapes. She'll remember their unique taste! She'll let you taste them. Is your grandmother from here?'

'Not exactly. Her grandparents went to Egypt, more than a hundred years ago. She lives in Europe.'

'What about you? You've got a different accent.'

'I'm from America.'

'USA, OK, Pepsi-Coca-Cola! I know! But you still have traces of your origins in your blood, even though you don't know it.'

'Do you think so? Ah! I'd like that!'

She clapped her hands.

'I am happy, happy!'

'You like it here?'

'I love it.'

This place was a real treasure trove and Aziz was a magician, so different from the hurried shopkeepers back at home. Despite the comings and goings of his customers, he always had time for Sybil, helping her to fill her bag and asking after Odette and Kalya.

The little girl often chose siesta time to go to the deserted shop. She would come across the shopkeeper snoozing on the counter or on the floor, leaning up against a sack of flour or rice. She would sit down beside him. They would jabber on for an hour and more, skipping from one language to another, waving their hands about and laughing.

It was a few days later, during the siesta, that the explosion occurred.

Before Odette or Kalya could stop her, the little girl tore downstairs and rushed towards the shop. Smoke billowed out.

Her hands pressed against what remained of the window, squashing her face up against the dusty glass, she had trouble making out, and then recognising Aziz's body, a soft, bloody, inert mass, slumped over the counter.

She went in, with searing heart.

The shelves, heavily laden, had collapsed onto a heap of rubble. Bits of wooden beams and old iron were mixed in with the debris.

Sybil approached the body. It was a nightmare, a horror film.

A crowd of local people had gathered in the square. Some, followed by Aziz's screaming parents, entered the shop through the gaping openings.

The little girl refused to believe what she saw. She wanted to touch her friend, wake him up. It was like one of those serials where the body, which is never completely dead, comes to life again the next day for the start of a new episode. She was convinced that Aziz would get up and once again take his place in the rebuilt shop. She could hear him already.

'It was a joke! Since I frightened you, you're entitled to a free Coca-Cola and some Suchard chocolate.'

Sybil had never encountered death, real death. In her country, death took place elsewhere; well out of sight, in hospital beds, in plane or car crashes. Bodies returned to air, or discreetly disappeared into varnished wooden coffins.

2   Write down three differences between Sybil's culture and the culture in Beirut.

3   What does this story suggest about experiencing different cultures?

4   How does the description of Aziz's shop and body after the explosion make you feel?

5   Why do you think the writer started the story by saying that the shop had been destroyed by a bomb?

Activity 2

1   Find quotations from the story that describe Aziz's appearance.

2   Find three sentences spoken by Aziz. What do they suggest about his character? One example has been done below.

'chubby face and round eyes'

Sentence spoken by Aziz	What it suggests about his character
'Drawer of the devil' shows Aziz talking to a drawer.	This makes Sybil laugh. It is funny as it suggests that Aziz is rather crazy talking to a drawer, and perhaps superstitious mentioning the devil.

3 The writer describes the shop as 'a treasure trove' and the shopkeeper as 'a magician'. What do these descriptions say about Sybil's feelings about her visits there?

4 Find a quotation describing the shop that creates a sense of magic and excitement.

5 Re-read the extract and then close the book. Imagine the city of Beirut. Draw a diagram like the one on the right, and add all the details that you can remember that made the culture and setting of Beirut seem exciting to Sybil.

the bazaar

Setting and culture

Beirut seems exciting to Sybil

Sharpen your skills · Subject-verb agreement

Read the passage below. Identify any errors in subject-verb agreement and correct them.

> An important moment in my childhood was the day I met my Uncle Tim. Tim live in Australia but he works all over the world with women in developing countries. He help them to understand setting up their own business. They learns how to become self-sufficient.

Assess your progress

1 Look again at the extract on pages 90–92. Choose a sentence that best describes Aziz's character and one that best describes Sybil's character. Explain your choice to a partner.

2 Look at the levels below. They focus on the skills of commenting on a writer's choice of language. Agree with your partner the level that best fits each of your responses.

Level 3	Level 4	Level 5
Say why one word is better than another	Explain why a writer might have chosen particular words	Comment on the significance of particular words and sentence styles
Notice the way sentences are written	Suggest possible effects on the reader of particular words and styles of sentences	Comment on the effects on the reader of particular words and styles of sentences

5 Reviewing a text

You are learning:
- to organise ideas in a sequence of paragraphs.

You have been developing your reading skills by looking at texts from different cultures. You now need to use these skills to write a review of *The Story of Sybil* on pages 90–92.

Activity 1

Here are some guidelines on how to structure a review.

| Introduction: What the story is called and what it is about | Paragraph 1: Details about the story setting and characters | Paragraph 2: Brief outline of features or themes | Paragraph 3: Reviewer's overall opinion of the story | Conclusion: Finish with idea of who the story might appeal to |

Now look at the sections of a story review below. Using the guidelines above, put the sections in order to structure a review for a reading website about good stories. Copy them out in your chosen order.

- My rating of the story and reasons for it.
- Who I would recommend this story to.
- The characters and my opinions about them.
- What the story is about.
- The setting and how the author helps the reader imagine it.
- The title and author of the story.
- Important issues or themes in the story (e.g. growing up, war).

Activity 2

A topic sentence is the first sentence of a paragraph. It gives an idea of what the paragraph is about. Write a topic sentence for each paragraph of the story review from Activity 1 above. For example:

- The characters and my opinions about them
  The two central characters in the story are Sybil and Aziz.

Activity 3

Use the planning you have done above to write a review of *The Story of Sybil* on pages 90–92. In each paragraph, use examples from the text to support your points and explain how the story describes a different culture.

Sharpen your skills — **The subject complement**

Aziz was a magician.

subject   verb   complement

The words *a magician* tell us more about the subject. They complete it, so they are called the complement of the sentence.

Write down whether the part of these sentences in **bold** is the complement or the object of the sentence.

- The explosion destroyed **the shop**.
- Aziz's shop was **a treasure trove**.

Assessment task

Reading: Understanding the author's craft

Lions in the night!

This extract is from a novel called *Forest of the Pygmies* by a Chilean novelist, Isabel Allende. In this novel, Kate, who is a writer, takes her grandson, Alexander, and his friend, Nadia, on safari to Kenya. Joel is a photographer and Mushaha is the guide for the safari.

Your task

Read the extract and then answer the questions that follow.

One night Kate is woken in her tent very suddenly.

Shortly before dawn Kate suddenly woke with alarm; she thought she had heard some noise very close by. 'I must have dreamed it,' she murmured, turning over on her cot. She tried to calculate how long she had slept. Her bones creaked, her muscles ached, and her legs were cramping. She felt every one of her sixty-seven hard-lived years; her frame was battered from her adventures. 'I'm too old for this kind of life,' the writer mused, but almost immediately retracted that thought, convinced that any other life was not worth living. She suffered more from lying in bed than from the fatigue of the day. The hours in the tent passed at a paralysing pace. Then again she heard the sound that had waked her. She couldn't identify it, but it sounded like a scraping or a scratching.

The last mists of sleep dissipated completely and Kate sat straight up in her cot, her throat dry and her heart pounding. No doubt about it; something was out there, just on the other side of the cloth tent. Very carefully trying not to make any noise, she felt in the darkness for her flashlight, which she always kept nearby. When she held it in her hand, she realised she was sweating with fear; her fingers were too moist to switch it on. She kept trying but was diverted when she heard the voice of Nadia, with whom she shared a tent.

'Shhh Kate! Don't turn on the light,' the girl whispered.

'What is it?'

'Lions. Don't be afraid,' Nadia answered.

The flashlight dropped from the writer's hand. She felt her bones turn to mush and a scream from her gut lodged in her throat. A single slash of a lion's claws would rip the thin nylon tent and the cat would be on them. It wouldn't be the first time a tourist had died that way on safari. During their treks they had seen lions so close that they could count their teeth; she had decided that she didn't care to meet them in the flesh. An image flashed through her mind; early Christians in the Roman Coliseum, condemned to be eaten alive by the beasts. Sweat ran down her face as she groped on the ground for the flashlight, by now entangled in the mosquito netting that hung around her cot. She heard the purring of a great cat and new scratchings.

This time the tent shook, as if a tree had dropped on it. Terrified, Kate dimly realised that Nadia was purring back. Finally she found the flashlight and with wet, trembling fingers she switched it on. She saw Nadia crouching down, her face against the cloth of the tent, enthralled, engaged in an exchange of deep purrs with the beast on the other side. The scream that had been stuck inside Kate escaped as a terrible howl that took Nadia by surprise, literally knocking her off her feet. Kate swept up the girl in one arm and began trying to pull her. New screams, this time accompanied by the chilling roars of the lions, shattered the quiet of the camp.

Within a few seconds, staff and visitors were outside, despite the specific instructions of Mushaha, who had warned them a hundred times of the dangers of leaving their tents at night. Kate was still tugging at Nadia, dragging her outside as the girl kicked and struggled, trying to get free. Half the tent collapsed in the tug of war, and one of the nettings broke loose and fell over them, enveloping them completely. They looked like two larvae trying to break out of a cocoon. Alexander, the first to arrive, ran to them and tried to untangle them from the netting. Once she was free, Nadia pushed him away, furious because her conversation with the lions had been interrupted in such an uncivilised fashion.

As that was going on, Mushaha fired his pistol into the air, and the roars of the lions faded into the distance. The guards lighted torches, sheathed their weapons, and set off to explore the area around the camp. By then the elephants were in an uproar, and their keepers were trying to calm them before they escaped their corrals and stampeded through the camp. Crazed by the smell of the lions, the three pygmy chimps were chattering and clinging to the first person who came by. Boroba had leaped onto Alexander, who was ineffectually trying to pull him off his head by tugging his tail. In all the confusion no one had any idea what had happened.

Joel had run outside yelling, his heart in his mouth.
'Snakes! A python!'
'Lions,' Kate corrected.
Joel stopped short, bewildered.
'It's not snakes?' He hesitated.
'No, only lions,' Kate repeated.
'And you woke me up for that?' sputtered the photographer.

---

1 Look again at paragraph 1. What woke Kate up?

2 What impression do you get of the life Kate has led, from paragraph 1? Support your ideas with references to the text.

3 How does the end of the first paragraph link back to the beginning of the first paragraph?

4 Draw up a table like the one below to explain Kate's feelings from the beginning of paragraph 2 ('The last mists of sleep...') to the end of paragraph 6 ('...and new scratchings').

The first one has been done for you.

Quotation	What this quotation shows about Kate's feelings
Kate sat straight up in her cot, her throat dry and her heart pounding.	Kate has woken up very suddenly and is instantly alert. Her 'dry throat' and 'pounding heart' show her body instinctively knows she is in danger.
When she held it in her hand she realised she was sweating with fear.	
She felt her bones turn to mush and a scream lodge in her throat.	
An image flashed through her mind; early Christians in the Roman Coliseum, condemned to be eaten alive by the beasts. Sweat ran down her face...	

5 How do these quotations show Kate's **increasing** fear in this part of the story?

6 Explain the difference between Kate's reactions to the lions and Nadia's reactions to the lions. Support your ideas with reference to the text.

7 How does the writer build up a sense of drama in paragraphs 7 and 8 (from 'This time...' to 'uncivilised fashion')? Refer to specific details in these paragraphs and comment on them.

8 'They looked like two larvae trying to break out of a cocoon'. What does the choice of language in this quotation suggest Kate and Nadia looked like?

9 In paragraph 9, how does the choice of language create an impression of noise and confusion? Refer to specific words and phrases from this paragraph and comment on them.

10 What is the impact of the ending of the story?

11 a What do you learn about the different characters' attitudes to the safari? Write a sentence about the different attitudes of each of the following characters, using a quotation to support your point:

Kate   Nadia   Joel   Mushaha

b Why do you think these characters have different attitudes? What might it tell you about their cultures?

6 Giving your views

You are learning:

- to decide on your own point of view, giving reasons for that viewpoint.

So far in this unit you have been looking at the features of writing from different cultures. You're now going to look more closely at your own culture: youth culture in Britain.

People often have very different views about youth culture. To decide on your own views about a topic you will need to consider other people's points of view and the reasons behind them.

Activity 1

1   Read the following two articles about youth culture: hoodies and the use of mobile phones by children.

http://www.raisingkids.co.uk

Hoodies Banned by Bluewater 12 May 2005

Shopping centre issues ban on teenage clobber

Britain's biggest shopping centre has issued a ban on youngsters wearing hooded tops. Bluewater Shopping Centre in Kent, which earlier this year was voted the country's most parent-friendly shopping experience, came up with the idea to stop kids from misbehaving. The company issued a 'zero tolerance approach to intimidating conduct' after shoppers complained about gangs of teenagers behaving badly.

The company's stance was supported today by Deputy Prime Minister John Prescott who told the BBC that hooded clothes were part of an 'intimidating' uniform. Bluewater has also banned the wearing of baseball caps and any other clothing which obscures the face and prevents problem youths being identified on CCTV.

2   Summarise the point of view of the Bluewater Shopping Centre in a sentence. Explain the reasons behind their point of view, in two or more bullet points.

← Point of view

← Reasons

http://www.tes.co.uk

Call to ban mobile phones from classrooms

Mobile phones should be classified as offensive weapons and pupils should be banned from using them in schools, according to a teachers' leader, PA News reports.

Chris Keates, general secretary of the NASUWT union, said teachers were being abused by pupils who target them via websites using images taken on mobile phone cameras.

She urged ministers at a meeting today to crack down on so-called 'cyberbullying'.

'Pupils who once had to content themselves with exhibiting poor behaviour when face to face with the teacher, now increasingly use technology from a distance to support their indiscipline,' she said.

'I have recently sent to ministers almost 100 cases of teachers being abused and bullied by mobile phones, emails and most frequently websites.

'These cases illustrate graphically the untold distress and trauma these websites cause. In my view they serve no useful purpose and should be closed down. These sites are fed by pupils' misuse of mobile phones.

'The time has come for mobiles in schools to be placed in the category of a potentially offensive weapon and action taken to prevent their use by pupils while on school premises.

'Regrettably, our evidence shows that some schools are still not taking these issues seriously. Firm action by the Government is needed now.'

---

3 Summarise the point of view of the teachers' union in a sentence. Explain the reasons behind their point of view using your own words, in two or more bullet points.

⟵ Point of view

⟵ Reasons

•

•

•

Activity 2

You can compare different viewpoints on a topic by looking at how extreme, moderate or relaxed they are.

1 Use a sliding-scale diagram like the one below to show different viewpoints on the topic of hoodies. The top and bottom statements show the most extreme viewpoints.

    a Think of any other points of view related to the topic.

    b Decide where these viewpoints fit on the sliding scale and add them in.

2 Use a sliding-scale diagram like the one above to show different viewpoints on the topic of mobile phones in schools.

    a Think of any other points of view related to the topic.

    b Decide where these viewpoints fit on the sliding scale and add them in.

3 Consider your own point of view on the topics of hoodies and mobile phones.

   a Mark your viewpoint on your sliding-scale diagrams from questions 1 and 2.

   b Write out your viewpoint next to your mark on the sliding-scale diagrams.

   c What are your reasons to support your viewpoint?

Sharpen your skills Pronouns (personal and possessive)

A personal pronoun can replace the noun in a sentence:

Daniel went to the shopping centre. ~~Daniel~~ took off his hoodie.
                                      He

Possessive pronouns show someone owns something:

That is ~~Chantelle's~~ mobile phone.
           her

1 Rewrite the paragraph below, replacing repeated nouns with pronouns to make the paragraph flow more easily.

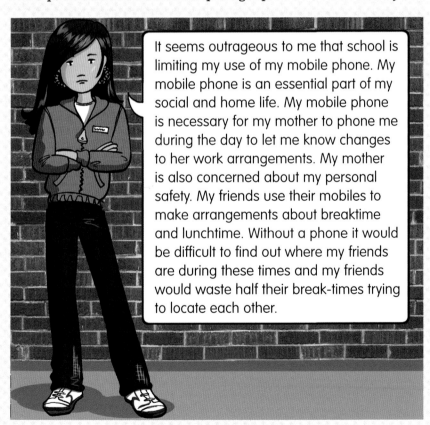

It seems outrageous to me that school is limiting my use of my mobile phone. My mobile phone is an essential part of my social and home life. My mobile phone is necessary for my mother to phone me during the day to let me know changes to her work arrangements. My mother is also concerned about my personal safety. My friends use their mobiles to make arrangements about breaktime and lunchtime. Without a phone it would be difficult to find out where my friends are during these times and my friends would waste half their break-times trying to locate each other.

2 Identify all the possessive pronouns in the paragraph.

7 Linking ideas

You are learning:
- to compare and contrast pairs of ideas about one issue.

Different people have different viewpoints on issues. When looking at an issue it is useful to compare and contrast the different points of view and reasons behind them.

Activity 1

1 Read the viewpoints from the parents' forum website below.

www.parentchatforum.com

Parent chat forum

Question: As parents, do you want your children to have mobile phones to take to school?

Parent 1

I am very concerned about the health concerns regarding mobile phones. Our GP advises parents not to let children use mobile phones, as in his opinion there is not enough proof that they cause no harm. Another disadvantage is the risk of the child being mugged for their phone.

Parent 2

My 16-year-old has a mobile phone that he uses on his way to school, at break or lunch. He often uses this to check with me by text whether he can stay for an after-school club and to speak to me after school. I have no problem with this. However should he ever be caught using his phone at school during lessons then I would not let him use it at school.

Parent 3

My child's school have embraced the use of mobile phones. They are making the most of technology that many children already have, and are using them in lessons as a technology device to take photographs and record voices.

Parent 4

It is important for all parents to realise the potential of mobile phones for bullying. My daughter has been a victim of harassment as a result of text messaging and pupils sharing photos. Schools should realise that these are dangerous tools for bullying.

Parent 5

Mobile phones are addictive and dangerous for children. Our daughter had been secretly using my credit card to buy airtime for her phone. We were very angry and worried. Mobile phone companies are clever in promoting the importance of social contact with friends as part of youth culture.

Parent 6

I am sure that many of you are aware of the issues related to exam cheating and mobile phones. As a teacher and a parent I think mobiles should not be allowed in school buildings.

2 Use a table like the one on the right to summarise the viewpoints for and against children having mobile phones in school.

For	Against

Activity 2

1 Look at the three statements below. For each statement add another **similar** point of view. Use appropriate connectives to join the statements, for example:

> Some parents think that mobile phones are a health risk, <u>similarly</u> others feel that they place the child at risk of being mugged.

a Some adults believe that mobile phones are addictive for teenagers…

b Many parents feel that mobile phones are essential for being able to monitor their children's safety…

c Some schools feel that mobile phones are valuable classroom resources…

2 Look at the following three statements. For each statement add another **contrasting** point of view. Use appropriate connectives to join the statements, for example:

> Some parents think that mobile phones have health risks, <u>whereas</u> others view them as essential safety devices.

a Mobile phones are viewed by some people as encouraging bullying…

b Some parents see mobile phones as important devices. They enable them to keep in contact with their children when they are not at home…

c Many schools have banned mobile phones because some children have used them to cheat in exams…

Sharpen your skills Connectives

Connectives join words, phrases or simple sentences together.

Connectives can add information, show contrast or show cause and effect. Use a table like the one below to sort the connectives in the word list.

Connectives for comparing	Connectives for contrasting
equally	whereas

similarly
likewise
alternatively
unlike
on the other hand
in the same way
instead of
as with
like
however
although

8 Organising ideas

You are learning:

- to use a variety of connectives to convey a personal viewpoint.

Companies choose certain viewpoints to promote their products or aims. For example, a company that sells sports equipment might take the view that everyone should play sport. There may be times when you want to respond to the viewpoint of a company, or an institution. You need to understand their viewpoint, think carefully about whether or not you agree with it, and then organise your response.

Activity 1

1 Read this website advertising Teddyfone, a mobile phone designed for children.

http://www.teddyfone.com

Teddyfone.com

The first ever safety phone for your children and grandchildren

Teddyfone menu

- Home
- About Teddyfone
- The Package
- Using Teddyfone
- Order Your Teddyfone
- Safety Factsheet
- Mobile Phone Usage
- Supporting Children's Charities
- Terms and Conditions
- Contact Us

Welcome to Teddyfone

Child safety is at the forefront of every parent's mind and as a result one in four children under 10 in the UK have a mobile phone. According to a recent report, parents believe that the benefits of giving children mobile phones (mobile parenting and safety) outweigh the negatives.

Faced with the dilemma of whether or not to give your child a mobile phone, for the first time you have a real choice, a **child safety phone** specifically designed to address the concerns about children's usage of mobile phones – the Teddyfone.

Main Features

- 10 times less emissions than a conventional mobile phone
- doesn't look like a mobile phone, so unlikely to attract unwanted attention
- limited functionality – no texting or downloading
- only allows calls to four preprogrammed numbers
- automated SOS alert feature
- child-tracking facility

2 Imagine you are a salesperson for the Teddyfone. What would you say to this grandmother to persuade her that the Teddyfone is the best option for her grandson? Remember to use examples to support your viewpoint and appropriate connectives from the list below to organise your ideas.

'Should I buy my 6-year-old grandson a mobile phone for his birthday?'

> **Connectives**
>
> **Comparing:** equally, in the same way, similarly, as with, like, just as, furthermore
>
> **Contrasting:** whereas, instead of, alternatively, otherwise, unlike, on the other hand
>
> **Using examples:** for instance, for example, such as, in the case of

Activity 2

Read the article below about one school's policy on mobile phones.

> Martin Edwards of the City of London High School says: 'We have a zero tolerance policy on mobile phones and other non-academic electronic equipment. They are not allowed in any circumstances. This is to discourage theft and the distraction they can cause during school hours.'

Imagine you are a parent who does not agree with the City of London Academy's policy on mobile phones. Write a letter to the school, expressing your point of view and the reasons behind it. Use examples to support your views and connectives from the list to organise your ideas.

Sharpen your skills Paragraphs

A paragraph is a group of sentences that are linked together.

Read the passage on the right, which is a review of the book below. Decide where a new paragraph should begin and give a reason why a new paragraph is needed.

Everything Bad is Good for You.

Why Popular Culture is Making Us Smarter

'As witty as Seinfeld and as wise as ER'
New Statesman

'Wonderfully entertaining'
Malcolm Gladwell

Steven Johnson

www.washingtonpost.com

Hello. My name is Bob, and I'm a Tetris addict. It's been eight years since I deleted the computer game from my hard drive, then frantically tried to retrieve it. Eight years since whole afternoons evaporated with nothing to show for them but eyestrain; eight years since I awakened from my Tetris trance to discover morning light leaking through my window. Now Steven Johnson informs me the experience made me stronger, and he has even better news for fans of today's more sophisticated games. In *Everything Bad Is Good For You*, Johnson is not talking about hand-eye coordination or reaction times. He claims that video games like SimCity and TV shows like *The Sopranos* give us a 'cognitive workout' that buffs the muscles between our ears. We're getting smarter, Johnson says, and the reason is the growing complexity – the multiple story threads and shifting interpersonal relationships – of the brain food flickering on our video screens. If only.

Assess your progress

Compare your writing from Activity 1 with a partner's. How confident are you in using connectives for comparing and contrasting: red, amber or green?

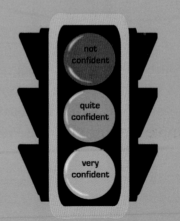

not confident

quite confident

very confident

Assessment task

Writing: Composition and conventions

School uniform around the world

Germany

There has been a lot of opposition to uniform for some time in Germany because of the Hitler Youth movement.

Japan

There is a very strict uniform in Japan: boys have to wear jackets (gakuran) and girls a dress called the sailor fuku, which is based on European naval uniform. The skirts have to be a particular length.

France

There is usually no uniform in state schools, but the wearing of Muslim headscarves and other 'conspicuous religious symbols' is banned.

Africa

Many children in Africa are proud to wear school uniform, but although its aim is to unify students, the poorest families can't afford it.

Australia

Uniform is compulsory in most schools in Australia: boys wear trousers and button-up shirts and girls wear dresses or skirts and blouses.

America

There is no uniform in most schools, though they usually have a dress code. Recently the number of schools with uniforms has increased, partly to prevent the wearing of 'gang clothing' or fights breaking out over which kind of trainers a student has.

Your school is going to review its policy on school uniform. You have been asked to consider different attitudes towards school uniform in countries across the world. This is to encourage parents, students and teachers to think about the advantages and disadvantages of wearing school uniform.

Your task

Write an article for your school magazine, analysing the advantages and disadvantages of wearing school uniform, commenting on school uniform in other countries, and giving your views on the subject.

In your article you should:

- analyse some of the advantages and disadvantages of wearing uniform
- explain which countries you think have the most sensible policies on uniform and why
- say whether you think uniform is a good idea for all school students or not.

Use some of the information and ideas on the resource sheet, as well as your own ideas.

Think about how you are going to make your article interesting for your readers – parents, students and teachers.

Remember to use a range of sentences with a variety of connectives to develop your ideas and make your writing interesting.

You don't have to use all the information and ideas you have been given.

Comments on uniform

'Uniforms make children feel part of a school community – they bring people together.'
– Headteacher

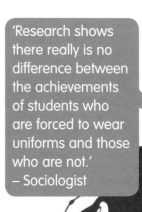

'Research shows there really is no difference between the achievements of students who are forced to wear uniforms and those who are not.'
– Sociologist

'I think uniform is a good idea but it can be very expensive, especially when children are growing rapidly.'
– Parent

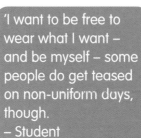

'I want to be free to wear what I want – and be myself – some people do get teased on non-uniform days, though.
– Student

5 Pen rhythm

Objectives

In this unit you will:

Reading
- identify and understand the main ideas and viewpoints in a text
- identify and describe the effect of a writers' use of language
- recognise and comment on the effect of writers' choices and techniques
- explore how the structure and presentation of a text help to create meaning.

Composition
- gather, select and organise ideas in a plan
- use evidence and opinions to develop your own point of view.

Conventions
- make plurals with -es, -y and -f endings
- learn to spell common homophones correctly
- increase your knowledge of regular spelling patterns.

Speaking and Listening
- summarise the most important points from a discussion
- have a successful discussion by listening and responding to the ideas of others.

By the end of this unit you will:

- select poems for a specific audience with assigned group roles (Speaking and Listening: Group discussion and interaction)
- analyse a poem by Benjamin Zephaniah (Reading: Understanding the author's craft).

Cross-curricular links

- **Citizenship**
  Identities and diversity: living together in the UK; issues and problems; environment

1 Poetic form

You are learning:
- how a poet can use form in poetry.

The **form** of a poem refers to its shape on the page. Sometimes poets write their poetry in the shape of the subject of the poem to give it visual impact.

Biography

Benjamin Zephaniah (1958–)
Benjamin Zephaniah was born in Handsworth, Birmingham and started creating his own poetry because he didn't like the poetry he was reading. His poems are about things that are important to him.

Activity 1

1 Read the poem.

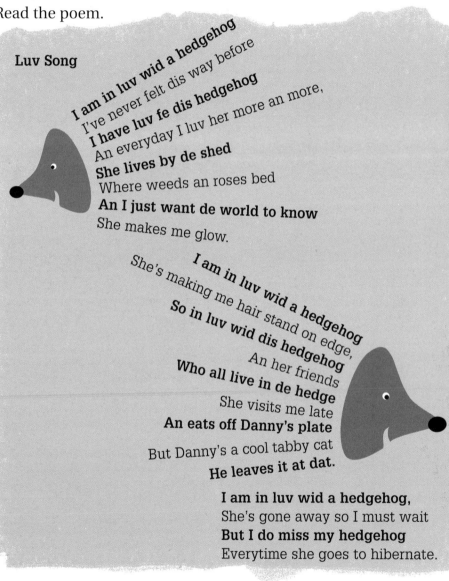

Luv Song

I am in luv wid a hedgehog
I've never felt dis way before
I have luv fe dis hedgehog
An everyday I luv her more an more,
She lives by de shed
Where weeds an roses bed
An I just want de world to know
She makes me glow.

I am in luv wid a hedgehog
She's making me hair stand on edge,
So in luv wid dis hedgehog
An her friends
Who all live in de hedge
She visits me late
An eats off Danny's plate
But Danny's a cool tabby cat
He leaves it at dat.

I am in luv wid a hedgehog,
She's gone away so I must wait
But I do miss my hedgehog
Everytime she goes to hibernate.

2 Now answer the following questions.
  a What events in Zephaniah's life might have inspired him to write the poem?
  b How is the poem set out on the page to link with the meaning?
  c Why are some lines printed in bold font? Choose from the possible reasons below:
   - To make us read them differently.
   - To help create the poem's shape.
   - Because it's a song.
   - To make them look like spines.

3 Read the last four lines again.

  a How are they similar to the other two stanzas?

  b How are they different?

  c Why do you think Zephaniah chose to write the poem in this way?

stressed

unstressed

Activity 2

In poetry, syllables help to create rhythm by creating patterns of beats. Some syllables are stressed and some are unstressed. This affects the way we say the words.

1 How many syllables are there in your name? For example, Julia has three syllables: Ju/li/a.

2 Look at this poem:

> Humpty Dumpty sat on a wall
> Humpty Dumpty had a great fall
> All the King's horses and all the King's men
> Couldn't put Humpty together again.

  a Read 'Humpty Dumpty' aloud and beat out its rhythm.

  b What do you notice about the number of beats in each line?

3 a Read the last four lines of 'Luv Song' again and count the syllables in each line.

  b Find the beats. What's the effect of the pattern?

Activity 3

Zephaniah often uses **dialect** in his poems so we can hear the sound and rhythm of his speech.

1 Find the words in 'Luv Song' that are dialect versions of:

love   the   with   my   for   that   and

Explanations

dialect the form of a language that is spoken in a particular place. For example the northern dialect word for alleyway is *ginnell*.

2 a Read the poem aloud, substituting standard English words for the dialect words. How does it sound? Which version do you prefer?

  b Why do you think the dialect words are spelt as they are?

3 Why do you think Zephaniah writes using Caribbean dialect?

2 Rhyme

You are learning:

● to appreciate the ways in which poets use rhyme.

When poetry rhymes, we say it has a **rhyme scheme**. This is the pattern made by the rhyme. To help us work out the pattern we give the rhyming sounds a name, such as a, b, c, d, etc.
When two lines next to each other rhyme, we call them a rhyming couplet.

Activity 1

1 Read Benjamin Zephaniah's poem 'The Vegans'. The rhyme scheme is shown for verse 1.

The Vegans

a	That man is really trying
a	To watch what he is buying,
b	So long as he is able
b	He will read every label,
c 5	He wants to know what's in
c	Each packet and each tin,
d	Before he hits the streets
d	He's checking out the eats.

That woman plants and grows
10 Then she reaps and she sows,
In order not to panic
She tries to eat organic,
She doesn't think she's perfect
But she thinks she is worth it,
15 She likes nice food that's memorable
Not bad food that's chemical.

Take a good look at that boy
Does he not fill you with joy?
He's trying to explain
20 That the thing he hates is pain,
That boy will never wear
Any fox fur or horsehair,
He will not follow fashion
His main thing is compassion.

25 That girl will not eat haddock
Or any animal product,
She's even learnt to think
About her bedtime drink,
She makes sure that her cuisine
30 Has the vitamins and protein
To keep her strong and healthy
Even if she is not wealthy.

2 Work out the rhyme scheme in verses 2, 3 and 4. Do you see any patterns?

Activity 2

Some of the rhymes in this poem rhyme exactly: *trying* and *buying*, for example. Some do not rhyme completely: *perfect* and *worth it*, for example. These are called half-rhymes.

1 Find three examples of half-rhyme in the poem.

2 Why do you think Zephaniah chose to use half-rhyme in the poem? Which do you think is the best one? Why?

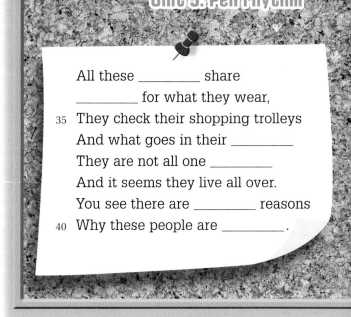

All these _____ share
_____ for what they wear,
35 They check their shopping trolleys
And what goes in their _____
They are not all one _____
And it seems they live all over.
You see there are _____ reasons
40 Why these people are _____ .

3 Choose two rhyming couplets from the poem. Use a thesaurus to help you rewrite the last word, keeping the same meaning but losing the rhyme. What difference have you made to the effect of the lines?

4 On the right is verse 5 of 'The Vegans', with some gaps. Choose some words to complete the poem.

Activity 3

Listen to someone reading the whole poem aloud.

1 Describe the effect of the rhyme. Try using some of the words below:

> lyrical   musical   balanced   bouncy   comical

2 a Sum up the whole poem in one sentence. You can use words or phrases from the poem.
b How do you think the poet feels or thinks about the people in the poem?
c What tone of voice should someone reading the poem use? Sad, happy, angry, or something else?
d How does the rhyme in the poem help create this mood or tone?

Sharpen your skills Common errors

Your means something belonging to someone. *You're* is short for *You are.*

Who's is short for *who is* or *who has.* *Whose* is a pronoun that is used when we ask who something belongs to.

Write the script of a conversation between two people.
Try to use *your*, *you're*, *whose* and *who's* four times each.

Assess your progress

Look carefully at your answers to Activities 2 and 3 and use the table below to see which level you are working at.

Level 3	Level 4	Level 5
I can refer to the shape of the poem on the page.	I can find the rhymes in the poem.	I can explain how the poet has used rhyme and rhythm in the poem.
I can explain what the poem is about.	I know what the poet thinks about food/animals.	I can explain, using examples, how the speaker feels about food/animals.

3 Rhyme and repetition

Poets often repeat words or phrases in poems to emphasise an important idea or a message. Repetition is often used to give a poem shape and create rhythm, which makes the important lines more memorable.

Activity 1

1 Read 'The Tourists are Coming' by Benjamin Zephaniah.

The Tourists are Coming

Tell them to be careful
If they're not give them an
  earful
The tourists are coming
The tourists are coming.

5 They may want to party
  nightly
But tell them they must
  be tidy
The tourists are coming
The tourists are coming.

They must respect what we've
  planted
10 They must not take us for
  granted
The tourists are coming
The tourists are coming.

They should practise what
  they preach
When they're lying on our
  beach
15 The tourists are coming to play.

Because our land is sunny
They come here with their
  money
The tourists are coming
The tourists are coming.

20 We will not rant and rave
If they will behave
The tourists are coming
The tourists are coming.

We will not be bitter
25 If they don't drop their litter
The tourists are coming
The tourists are coming.

If they don't mess about
We will not kick them out
30 The tourists are coming
  to stay.

If by chance you see some
Try to make them welcome
The tourists are coming
The tourists are coming.

35 If they treat us good
They're welcome in the
  neighbourhood
The tourists are coming
The tourists are coming.

But if they're out of order
40 Show them to the border
The tourists are coming
The tourists are coming.

And if it does start raining
Tell them off if they're
  complaining
45 The tourists are coming
  I say.

Tell them that we love living
And money can't buy
  everything
The tourists are coming
The tourists are coming.

50 Call them names like fools
  and criminals
If they don't respect our
  animals
The tourists are coming
The tourists are coming.

Tell them if they can't keep the
  peace
55 That tourism may have to
  cease
The tourists are coming
The tourists are coming.

Tell them not to be greedy
And be careful where they wee
  wee
60 The tourists are coming
  this way.

2 Choose a rhyming couplet from the poem. Draw an image to represent its meaning. For example, for lines 1 and 2 you could draw someone pouring a jug labelled 'complaints' into an ear.

3 Perform a reading of the poem as a whole class. Hold up your image when you read your chosen couplet.

4 Try to think of a movement or gesture to go with your chosen couplet. Perform the poem again, using your movement or gesture when you read your lines.

Activity 2

1 Who is the speaker in the poem talking to?

2 What does the speaker think about tourists? Choose from the list below or think of an idea of your own.

- He welcomes tourists.
- He hates tourists.
- He likes tourists who protect the environment.
- He likes quiet tourists.
- He needs the income from tourism.
- He wants to stop tourism.

Activity 3

1 Zephaniah repeats the line 'The tourists are coming' in every verse, sometimes with some changes. Why does he do this? Is it to:

- create rhythm?
- make it feel as if the tourists are coming any minute now?
- make it sound as if everyone is talking about it?
- make the poem longer?
- make it seem as if lots of tourists are coming?

2 Think of as many nursery rhymes as you can.
   a Which of them use a similar rhyme scheme to the poem?
   b Which have a regular rhythm like 'The Tourists are Coming'?
   c Which use repetition?

3 Why has Zephaniah used similar techniques to nursery rhymes in this poem?

Activity 4

1 Did the poem make you laugh? When?

2 What is the tone or mood of this poem? Would you describe it as angry? Polite? Comic? Serious? A warning?

3 What makes you think this? How do the rhyme, rhythm and repetition help create this feeling?

4 Active reading

You are learning:
- to use active reading strategies to make sense of texts.

One of the most exciting things about poetry is that there are so many meanings to be found within each poem. As long as we can explain our ideas about what a poem might mean and support them with evidence, then our ideas are valid.

Activity 1

1 Read Benjamin Zephaniah's poem 'For Sale' and think about the form in which it is written.

For Sale

Looking for a bargain
Come on down
It's the sale of the century
Look around
5 There are sights to see
And places to be
With way out cosmic activity
This is a deal you can't refuse
The kind of bet you cannot lose
10 So come on down
The price is right
I got to sell this thing tonight.

Chorus
Roll up, Roll up, Planet for Sale
Roll up, Planet for Sale.
15 Free of living things that roam
Free of people and ozone
I invite you to test my ware
Free of any atmosphere.

Enjoy yourself as you get poorly
20 With no sign of a creepy crawly
I promise you will find no trees
And no flowers to make you sneeze.
Little Bo Peep has gone with her sheep
And Little Jack Horner dissolved in a corner,
25 That Donald Duck
Has run out of luck
And Paddington
Bear is no longer here
The Owl and the Pussy Cat went to sea
30 Then got lost in infinity.
Alive Alive no, Alive Alive no
Cockles and Mussels are not, and no snow.

Chorus
Roll up, Roll up, Planet for Sale
Roll up, Planet for Sale.
35 Looking for a bargain, check this planet
Not a thing is moving on it
Just for you I'll do a deal
I'll swap it for a decent meal.

2 **a** What point is the speaker making in the poem?
   b Why does the poet use a chorus?
   c What is your response to the poem?

Activity 2

1 Look at these words and phrases taken from the poem:

> no flowers   sale   dissolved   bet   sell   bargain   gone   deal   got lost

Think of two categories into which you could sort all these words and phrases.
What does this suggest about the point the poet is making?

2 Write down three positive statements from the poem. Write a sentence or two explaining why you think the poet chose to include them.

3 Write down three negative statements from the poem. Write a sentence or two explaining why you think the poet chose to include them.

Activity 3

1 The poem mentions some familiar characters from stories and rhymes:

- Little Bo Peep
- Jack Horner
- Donald Duck
- Paddington Bear
- the Owl and the Pussy Cat.

What do you know about these characters? Use a table like the one below to record your ideas about what Zephaniah says about them and why he uses them in this poem.

Character	What do I know about this character?	Why does Zephaniah use this character in the poem 'For Sale'?
Little Bo Peep		
Jack Horner		
Donald Duck		
Paddington Bear		
the Owl and the Pussy Cat		

2 Read the last two lines of the poem.
  a Who is the speaker talking to?
  b Why do they ask for a meal?
  c How do you know this?

3 The seller in the poem makes some surprising statements, such as:
- Enjoy yourself as you get poorly
- I promise you will find no trees

Explain what you find surprising about these lines.

Activity 4

Write three questions to help someone explore the poem. Try to use questions that will help them think about the decisions the poet took when writing the poem. They could begin:
- Why has Benjamin Zephaniah…?
- What is the effect of…?

5 Poetic techniques

You are learning:
● how poetic techniques are used to create visual and sound effects and to help readers understand the poet's feelings and ideas.

Poets use techniques like simile, metaphor, personification and alliteration to bring out images and sounds in their poems.

Activity 1

A **simile** is used to compare one thing with another using the words 'like' or 'as'.

They fight like cat and dog.

she's as cool as a cucumber.

In 'Urdu Poets' Benjamin Zephaniah uses some powerful imagery. In the first stanza he writes:

Urdu poets speak wonders,
They are like magical wordsmiths,
They pluck words out of the sky
And create something for you to live for.

1   Find the simile in the first stanza of 'Urdu poets'.

Urdu poets

Urdu poets have a heavenly language
A language created by poets for poets,
A language that has turned a nation into poets,
5 Poets that love to speak to each other.
They bring glory to the bazaars,
Hope to the pavements
Libraries to the mind,
They light up dark wordless days
10 Adding joy to eyes that are sad.
Urdu poets have been known to create paradise in downtown Karachi

And wordplay on cricket fields,
Their verse so full of grace
15 Even when it is angry Urdu is beautiful.
Combine fire with water combine the calm with the storm,
Combine the greatest painters
With the greatest subjects
20 And you will have Urdu Poets.
Knowledge can be tasty.
To question can be delightful.

2   What is Zephaniah trying to say about Urdu poets?

Activity 2

1   Write down two metaphors that are commonly used.

A **metaphor** is used to suggest that one thing is like another thing. Instead of using *like* or *as*, it says that one thing *is* another thing.

'Your room is a tip!'

2 Poets use metaphor to create vivid images.
In his poem, Zephaniah says that Urdu poets:

> *bring glory to the bazaars,*
> *Hope to the pavements*
> *Libraries to the mind.*

a What do these metaphors suggest?
b Why do you think Zephaniah chose these metaphors?
c Try to rewrite these three lines without using metaphors.

Activity 3

Personification is when something that is not alive is given human characteristics. It can be used to create atmosphere and descriptive detail in writing.

The sun peeped over the hills and smiled on the valley below.

Think about the qualities given to the sun in this cartoon. Choose from the words in the box below to describe the atmosphere created by the personification.

spooky	gloomy	tense
menacing	violent	mysterious
happy	positive	warm

Activity 4

Alliteration is the effect created when words that start with the same sound are placed close together.

Make a list of advertising slogans that use alliteration.

Summer Sizzles on!

Grumpy Grandpa Gets Even!

Assess your progress

You are learning to use the terms for analysing imagery. Decide which level you think you are working at and what your target for improvement is.

Level 3	Level 4	Level 5
I can identify some imagery.	I can identify imagery and comment on what it means.	I can identify imagery and make comments about its effectiveness.

Sharpen your skills Common errors

Some words sound the same or similar but have different spellings and meanings. Write a sentence for each word to show you understand its meaning.

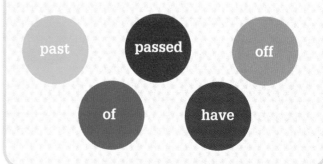

past · passed · off · of · have

6 Language choices

Writers use emotive words to show how strongly they feel they have about something.

Activity 1

1 Read the poem 'No Problem' by Benjamin Zephaniah.

No Problem

I am not de problem
But I bare de brunt
Of silly playground taunts
An racist stunts,
5 I am not de problem
I am a born academic
But dey got me on de run
Now I am branded athletic,
I am not de problem
10 If yu give I a chance
I can teach yu of Timbuktu
I can do more dan dance,
I am not de problem
I greet yu wid a smile
15 Yu put me in a pigeon hole
But I am versatile.

These conditions may affect me
As I get older,
An I am positively sure
20 I hav no chips on me shoulders,
Black is not de problem
Mother country get it right,
An juss fe de record,
Sum of me best friends are white.

2 Who is speaking in this poem?

3 Zephaniah uses emotive language in the poem to show how he feels about racism. Here are some examples:

taunts   racist   on de run

problem   branded   bear de brunt   silly

a What do these words make you think about?
b What point does Zephaniah make about racism?

4 Look at these three metaphors from the poem:

on de run   **pigeon hole**   **Mother country**

What do you think these metaphors suggest?

Activity 2

1 Read the last two lines of the poem again. Why did the poet end the poem with these words?
   a To end the poem on a light-hearted note.
   b To show the speaker has no hard feelings.
   c You think the poem is finished and these two lines are a surprise.
   d He's showing he is not racist.

2 Why do you think Zephaniah chose to write this poem in dialect?

3 Write a set of stage directions, explaining to an actor how you think this poem should be read aloud. Think about which words or phrases should be emphasised, where there should be pauses, where it should be loud or quiet and the tone in which it should be read.

Sharpen your skills Common errors

Some words sound the same or similar but have different spellings and meanings.

1 Write out the following sentences, inserting the correct word.

there   their   they're

   a   The children put _____ shoes in the cupboard.
   b   'We mustn't disturb them, _____ too small at the moment,' said Dad.
   c   In the box under the stairs _____ were six tiny black and white kittens.

2 Write out the following sentences and fill in the correct words.

where   were   we're

   a   'Do you know _____ my new scarf is?' asked Mum.
   b   'We put it in the box with the kittens because they _____ cold,' admitted Jake.
   c   'When we come home from school, _____ going to name them,' he continued.
   d   Meanwhile, the kittens _____ purring contentedly in their warm bed.

7 Looking at audience

You are learning:
- to understand how audiences and readers choose and respond to texts.

When we read we bring our own understanding and experience to that reading, so we often see different things. It is interesting to hear how other people interpret poems so we can deepen our own understanding.

Activity 1

1   Read the following extracts from some year 7 students' writing about Benjamin Zephaniah's poems.

(A) In 'The Tourists are Coming' the locals are talking. They want to remind the tourists about how to treat their beaches and countryside. *Adam*

(B) My favourite poem is 'The Vegans'. If I wanted to make a presentation of this poem, I would add some music to emphasise the beat. *Chelsea*

(C) In 'No Problem', Zephaniah wants us to think about racist bullying. *Stephen*

(D) This poem ('The Vegans') is special to Benjamin Zephaniah because he is a vegan. *Rhea*

(E) I liked 'Luv Song' because it was funny and the hedgehog seemed almost human. *Ellen*

(F) I think 'No Problem' has the most serious message. *Ben*

2   Do you agree or disagree with these statements? Explain your reasons, using evidence from the poems to support your answer.

3 Which poem have you enjoyed the most? Write a paragraph of three or four sentences about the poems you have read so far. Try and include a line from a poem in your response. Use some of these sentence starters:

- I agree with the person who says '_____' because _____
- When the poet says '_____' it makes me think about _____
- I like the sound of the rhyme in this poem because _____
- This poem made me wonder why _____
- The line '_____' makes me feel that the poet thinks _____
- The ending of the poem suggests to me that _____

4 Find out which poems other people in your class enjoyed the most and why they liked them. Is there a class favourite?

Activity 2

Working in a group, you are going to choose your favourite poem from the ones you have studied and give a presentation on it. You can use this structure:

1 Introduce the poem. What is it about?
2 The reason we picked this poem is…
3 The best line or phrase in the poem is… because…
4 I think the poet was trying to make me think or feel that…
5 The poem made me think or feel that…

When you rehearse and give your presentation, think about the way in which you will get your message across to the audience. Think about pace, volume, gesture, expression and eye contact.

Assess your progress

As you watch and listen to other groups' presentations, use the table below to decide which level they are working at. For each group, note one thing you think they did well and one thing that they could improve on to achieve a higher level.

Level 3	Level 4	Level 5
I can take part in a group presentation.	I can take an active part in a group presentation.	I can use different techniques to engage an audience.
I listen carefully to the comments made by others.	I can suggest ideas to make a presentation interesting for an audience.	I can evaluate the work of others using some appropriate words such as: pace, gesture, etc.

Assessment task

Speaking and Listening: Group discussion and interaction

Poetry Performance!

Your class has been asked to put on a poetry performance for Year 6 students. In groups, choose six poems that go together well, perhaps with a common theme, and decide how you are going to perform them.

Your task

Prepare a poetry performance for Year 6 students. You should:

- choose a theme for your performance
- select six poems to perform
- decide how you are going to introduce your show and how you are going to perform your final poem.

What to do:

1 Choose a theme that Year 6 students will enjoy and find interesting and poems that are suitable for performing.

2 Use poems from this book, other books in the library, the Internet or books you have at home. They could be by one poet or different poets.

3 Your introduction should make your show sound interesting and exciting. Annotate your last poem with notes about how it should be performed.

You will be assessed on how well you work together as a group:

- listening to each other

- coming to an agreement

- making suggestions

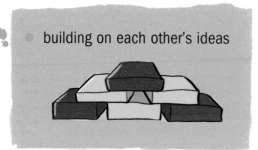

- building on each other's ideas

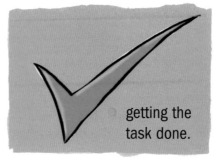

- getting the task done.

8 A writer's point of view

You are learning:
- to identify and comment on a writer's purpose and viewpoint, and the overall effect of the text on the reader.

Poems are written for many different reasons. The poet may wish to express strong feelings or a particular point of view.

Activity 1

1   Read the poem 'The British' by Benjamin Zephaniah.

The British
(serves 60 million)

Take some Picts, Celts and Silures
And let them settle,
Then overrun them with Roman conquerors.

5   Remove the Romans after approximately 400
     years
Add lots of Norman French to some
Angles, Saxons, Jutes and Vikings, then stir
     vigorously.

Mix some hot Chileans, cool Jamaicans,
     Dominicans,
Trinidadians and Bajans with some Ethiopians,
     Chinese,
10 Vietnamese and Sudanese.

Then take a blend of Somalians, Sri Lankans,
     Nigerians
And Pakistanis,
Combine with some Guyanese
And turn up the heat.

15 Sprinkle some fresh Indians, Malaysians,
     Bosnians,
Iraqis and Bangladeshis together with some
Afghans, Spanish, Turkish, Kurdish, Japanese
And Palestinians
Then add to the melting pot.
20 Leave the ingredients to simmer.

As they mix and blend allow their languages
     to flourish
Binding them together with English.

Allow time to be cool.

Add some unity, understanding and
     respect for the future
25 Serve with justice
And enjoy.

Note: *All the ingredients are equally important.
Treating one ingredient better than another
will leave a bitter, unpleasant taste.*

30 ***Warning:*** *An unequal spread of justice will
damage the people and cause pain. Give
justice and equality to all.*

2 Look at the statement in the table below. Which statements match your understanding of what the poet is saying in 'The British'? Find lines from the poem to support the statements.

Statement	Is the poet saying this in the poem?	Line in the poem supporting statement
All people deserve to be treated with respect.		
It takes time for people to live in harmony.		
We have to work at getting along with all kinds of people.		
Throughout history the population has changed.		
Everyone is equal.		
It's exciting to live in a multicultural society.		
Benjamin Zephaniah is passionate about justice and equality.		

3 The Romans, Angles, Saxons, Jutes and Normans all came to Britain hundreds of years ago. What point do you think Benjamin Zephaniah is making by including them in the poem?

Activity 2

1 The poem is written like a recipe.

Hot Herb Bread

Ingredients

1 French loaf

90g softened butter

2 crushed garlic cloves (if you like)

1 tablespoon chopped parsley

1 tablespoon snipped chives

1 Oven setting:
200C/400F/Gas mark 6

2 Mix the butter, herbs and garlic together.

3 Make cuts along the loaf but do not cut right through it.

4 Spread both sides of each cut with herb butter.

5 Wrap the loaf in foil. Bake it for 10–15 minutes

6 Eat the bread hot. It tastes wonderful with salad.

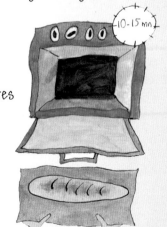

a What words and other features in 'The British' make the poem like a recipe?

b Why has Zephaniah chosen to write this poem like this? Use the following sentence prompts:

- Zephaniah wants to show that Britain has become a multicultural society so he _____
- The poem is set out like a recipe. It starts with _____
- The words 'stir vigorously' make me think that _____
- When he uses the words 'melting pot' Zephaniah wants us to think _____
- Zephaniah uses the word 'blend' to suggest _____
- When he writes: 'And turn up the heat' Zephaniah could mean that _____
- When he says 'And enjoy' Zephaniah means that _____

2 Re-read the note and the warning at the end of the poem. Why has Zephaniah included them? Was it because:
- sometimes recipes carry a warning about the meal?
- the note allows him to express his feelings more forcefully?
- he wants to reinforce his message about justice and equality?

Write a paragraph to explain your answer. You can use the following structure:
- Make your point: I think that Zephaniah included the note and the warning at the end of the poem because...
- Use a quote from the poem as evidence to support your point.
- Write a sentence or two explaining how your evidence supports your point.

Assess your progress

Look at the work you have completed on the poem 'The British'. Which level are you working at? Decide what you have to do to improve.

Level 3	Level 4	Level 5
I know what the poem is about.	I can comment on the writer's point of view.	I can comment on the writer's point of view and give some explanation of his viewpoint, using examples from the poem to support my ideas.

9 Writing about poems

You are learning:
● to write about a poem.

When we write about poems we need to explain what we think. By choosing words or phrases from the poem we can support our ideas.

Activity 1

1   Read the poem 'Pets Control' by Benjamin Zephaniah.

Pets Control

We moved into a house
We kicked de animals out,
Den we got our pets
An signed on at de vets,
5 We den called wild life strays
Zoos captured dem,
We gazed,
Wild life made great TV,
How civilised were we?

2   **a**   List the different groups of animals mentioned in the poem.
     b   Describe the ways in which these different groups are treated?

3   **a**   There is a question at the end of the poem. Why do you think Zephaniah does this?
     b   What is your answer to Zephaniah's question?

Activity 2

When we write about poetry, it's useful to have a structure we can remember to record our ideas. Try using SMILE, which means:

Structure and form – how the poem is written, set out on the page and how this links to
Meaning – what the poem is about and what makes you think that
Imagery – the use and effects of simile, metaphor and personification
Language – words and phrases which you think are important, powerful or puzzling
Explain your ideas – use words or phrases to support your ideas.

Read 'Pets Control' again. Use a table like the one below to record your ideas. Some sentence starters are included to help you.

Your thoughts	'Pets Control'
Structure and form	The short lines like '...' made me think ...
Meaning	
Imagery	'we kicked de animals out'. The word 'kicked' made me feel...
Language (pick out key words and phrases)	
Explain your own ideas, likes and dislikes about the poem	My favourite line is '...'. The poet seems to be saying that...

Activity 3

1   Find the point, the example and the explanation in the example above.

2   Using the notes from your table, develop detailed sentences explaining your thoughts about the poem. Remember to use words or phrases from the poem. Make a point, use an example and then explain your idea. Read this example:

Point ⟶ | Zephaniah varies the line lengths in 'Pets Control': | 'We gazed' is

Evidence ⟶ much shorter than the other lines, | so when I read the poem it made

Explain ⟶ me pause and think because 'gaze' suggests looking at something for

a long time like we do when we stare at animals in the zoo.

Assess your progress

Look at your partner's sentences from Activity 3. Work out which is the point, which is the example and which is the explanation. Check that each does the job it should.

● Does the point identify a key feature of the poem?

● Does the example use a quotation from the poem to support the point?

● Does the explanation comment on how the evidence supports the point? Does it comment on the effect it has on the reader?

Sharpen your skills Plurals

When you make a noun into a plural you usually add -s or -es to the end of the word.

-s
book – books, lock – locks

-es (words that end in -s, -z, -x, -ch or -sh
church – churches
brush – brushes
loss – losses
Think of words that end in -s, -z, -x, -ch or -sh and write them in the plural.

10 Planning

When you note down your ideas after reading a poem, your notes may not be very organised. This can make it difficult to express your thoughts clearly. However, you can make a plan to help you choose the main points you wish to make and think about the best order in which to present them.

Activity 1

1   Below is a jumbled-up version of a plan for a piece of writing about 'The Vegans' by Benjamin Zephaniah (see page 112). Organise the points into the best order.

> **A** Each verse describes a person who is careful about what they eat.

> **B** The last two lines seem as if the poet is answering the question, 'Why do people become vegans?'.

> **C** The rhyming couplets give the poem a bouncy rhythm that sounds positive.

> **D** The poem is about people's concerns about animals.

> **E** Finally, I enjoyed this poem most of all because it made me think about what I eat.

> **F** The poet uses standard English and it seems as if he is talking to us at the supermarket.

Use the essay structure below to help you decide which point should go in which paragraph.
*   **Paragraph 1**: What is the poem about?
    Paragraph 2: How is the poem structured or organised?
*   **Paragraph 3**: What kind of language does the poet use?
*   **Paragraph 4**: How has the poet used rhyme and rhythm?
*   **Paragraph 5**: What was the poet's intention in writing this poem?
*   **Paragraph 6**: What is your response to this poem?

2   Using your notes and the essay structure, write the first sentence of each paragraph to explain your ideas about 'Pets Control'.

Activity 2

1   Take each of your points and develop them into a paragraph containing two or three sentences using Point–Example–Explain.

2   When you write your conclusion in the final paragraph, make sure you refer back to a point you made in your opening paragraph. You should also try to add something to that point, to round off your essay and explain why you responded as you did.

Activity 3

Connectives help you link ideas both within and between paragraphs. Look at this example, which compares the two poems 'The Vegans' and 'No Problem':

'In 'The Vegans', Zephaniah uses standard English <u>which</u> makes it sound as if he is talking to us at the supermarket as we watch the shoppers. <u>However</u> in 'No Problem' on page 120, he uses non-standard English <u>which</u> creates a different voice.'

Try adding some of these connectives to each of your paragraphs:

To contrast different things in the poems

On the other hand...
Whereas...
However...

To tell the reader where they are in the essay

First...
Finally...
In conclusion...

To introduce examples

For example...
For instance...
...such as...

To introduce explanations

This shows that...
This suggests that...
This implies that...

To compare similar things in the poems

Similarly...
In the same way...
Equally...

Assess your progress

Level 3	Level 4	Level 5
I can express an opinion about the text	I can group similar ideas together	I can link paragraphs
I can choose words or phrases from the text	I can organise ideas logically	I can explain ideas in detail using textual references

Check your writing about the poems. Decide which level you are working at and what you need to do to improve.

Sharpen your skills – Plurals

Words that end in -y in the singular are made plural by dropping the -y and adding -ies, as in: *pony – ponies, trophy – trophies*.

Words that end in -ey in the singular are made plural by adding an -s, as in: *monkey – monkeys*.

Words that end in -f in the singular are usually made plural by dropping the -f and adding -ves as in: *half – halves* or by adding -s as in: *belief – beliefs*

Write a test for a partner listing the singular form of six words that end in -y, -ey or -f. Your partner's task is to turn them all into plurals.

Assessment task

Reading: Understanding the author's craft

Mothers and sons

These two poems are about mothers and sons. The first is by Benjamin Zephaniah; the second is by Langston Hughes.

Your task

Read the poems and answer the questions that follow.

I Love me Mudder

I luv me mudder an me mudder luvs me
We cum so far from over de sea,
We heard dat de streets were paved wid gold
Sometimes it's hot, sometimes it's cold,
5 I luv me mudder an me mudder luvs me
We try fe live in harmony
Yu might know her as Valerie
But to me she's just my mummy.

She shouts at me daddy so loud sometime
10 She's always been a friend of mine
She's always doing de best she can
She works so hard down ina Englan,
She's always singin sum kinda song
She has big muscles an she very, very strong,
15 She likes pussycats an she luvs cashew nuts
An she don't bother wid no if an buts.

I luv me mudder an me mudder luvs me
We come so far from over de sea,
We heard dat de streets were paved wid gold
20 Sometimes it's hot, sometimes it's cold,
I luv her and whatever we do
Dis is a luv I know is true,
My people, I'm talking to yu
Me an my mudder we luv yu too.

1 In line 3 of his poem, Zephaniah says that he and his family expected the streets to be 'paved wid gold'. What do you think they expected England to be like?

2 Zephaniah uses dialect in this poem. Find two examples and explain what effect each of them has.

3 In the second verse, almost every line begins in the same way. Why do you think Zephaniah chose to do this? What effect does it have?

4 Try to imagine how 'I Luv me Mudder' would sound if someone read it aloud. What do you notice about the rhythm of the poem? What effect does the rhythm have?

5 Zephaniah says he loves his mother. What other feelings does he have towards her?

6 What do you notice about the three verses of 'I Luv me Mudder'? Sum up what each verse is about.

7 What do you notice about the order of the verses?

Mother to Son

Well, son, I'll tell you:
Life for me aint been no crystal stair
It had tacks in it
And splinters,
5 And boards torn up
And places with no carpet on the floor –
Bare.
But all the time
I'se been a climbin' on,
10 And reaching landin's,
And turning corners,
And sometimes goin' in the dark
Where there aint been no light.
So boy, don't you turn back.
15 Don't you set down on the steps
'Cause you find it's kinda hard.
Don't you fall now –
For I'se still goin', honey,
I'se still climbin',
20 And life for me aint been no crystal stair.

8 Who is speaking in 'Mother to Son'?

9 In Hughes's poem, the mother compares her life to stairs in a house. What do you think she means when she says her life 'aint been no crystal stair'?

10 The following quotations all suggest something about Hughes's mother's life. Complete a table like the one below, explaining what you think each one means. One has been done for you.

Quotation	What this quotation suggests about the mother's life
It had tacks in it	'Tacks' are like nails, and suggests that there have been hard things that have made her life difficult at times
And places with no carpet on the floor	
I'se been a climbin' on	
And sometimes goin' in the dark	

11 What is the effect of putting the word 'Bare' on its own on a line at this point in 'Mother to Son'?

12 Explain the advice that Hughes's mother gives him. Support your ideas by referring to the poem.

13 This question is about both poems. It asks you to compare the way the two mothers are presented by Zephaniah and Hughes.

Answer each part of the question by completing tables like the ones below.

a What impression do you get of each mother?

The mother in 'I Luv Me Mudder'	The mother in 'Mother to Son'

b How are the two mothers similar and how are they different?

The similarities between the two mothers	The differences between the two mothers

c How are the two poems similar in the way they are written and how are they different?

Similarities between the way the two poems are written	Differences between the way the two poems are written

You could end by explaining which poem you prefer and why.

6 Take action

Objectives

In this unit you will:

Reading
- use skimming and scanning to find relevant information from a text
- make relevant notes when gathering ideas from texts
- explore how writers organise, structure and present texts.

Writing
- use evidence and opinions to develop your own point of view
- use colons and semi-colons accurately
- organise ideas into a sequence of paragraphs
- use well-structured paragraphs and a range of linking words and phrases to make your ideas clear
- proofread and revise a piece of writing to improve it.

Conventions
- choose an appropriate level of formality
- understand and use pronouns and complex and compound sentences
- increase your knowledge of word families and regular spelling patterns such as prefixes and vowel choices.

Speaking and Listening
- identify the key features of a speech
- summarise the most important points from a talk and a discussion.

By the end of this unit you will:

- analyse a final speech (Speaking and Listening: Listening and responding)
- create a leaflet to present a group's views (Writing: Composition and conventions).

Cross-curricular links

- **Citizenship**
  Critical thinking and enquiry: environment; advocacy and representation

1 Finding information

You are learning:

● to understand how information can be presented and how to find the information you need.

We pick up information not just through words but from pictures, presentational features and the way in which they are organised.

Activity 1

The web page below is from the Recycling Guide website. This is a national campaign that encourages us to recycle our rubbish and help the environment.

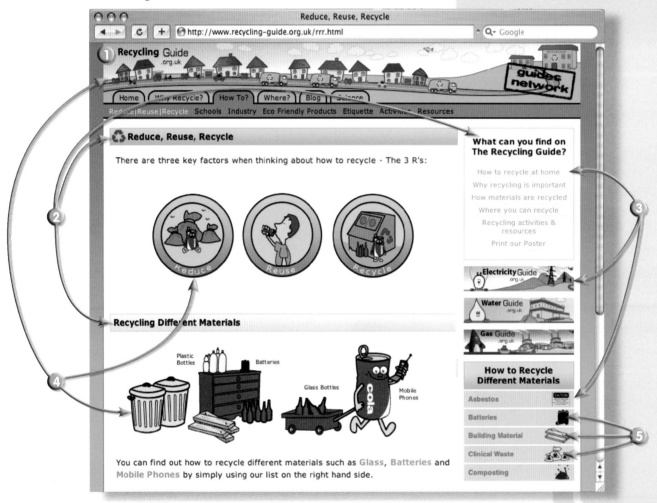

1 Look at the presentational features listed in the box opposite that the website designer has used to attract the reader and organise the information. Match the features to the numbered arrows.

2 What responses was the designer trying to create in the reader? Write a sentence about each feature to explain your answer.

a **Links to other pages on the site**
b **Headings**
c **The name of the campaign**
d **Images**
e **Coloured text boxes**

Activity 2

It's the summer holidays. You're bored. You have persuaded a parent to take you to a theme park. They have agreed, but on the condition that you do all the organising.

Write down where you could find the answer to each of the following questions.

- I want to go tomorrow. What will the weather be like?
- What's the best way to get there?
- How much will it cost?
- The theme park's website says the café has been *refurbished*. What does that mean?

Activity 3

There are lots of ways of organising information. Look at the following three texts and answer the questions to practise your information-finding skills.

Text 1 is taken from a leaflet to encourage recycling:

Text 1

Over 50% of the rubbish in our bins can be recycled, and yet:

♻ 74% of waste goes to landfill. This generates dangerous liquids and gases. Many landfill sites are nearly full and we are running out of suitable land to build new sites.

♻ 18% of waste is recycled – this saves landfill space, energy, import costs and raw materials. It also cuts air pollution.

♻ 8% of waste is incinerated – this produces smoke, ash and dangerous chemicals such as dioxins, but usually in amounts so small that they are not dangerous.

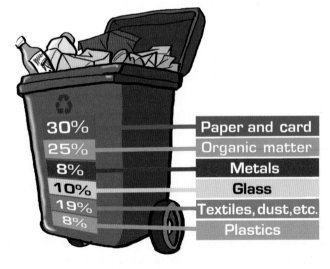

The average household bin contains:

30%	Paper and card
25%	Organic matter
8%	Metals
10%	Glass
19%	Textiles, dust, etc.
8%	Plastics

1 Diagrams can give the reader a lot of information.
   Use the diagram above to work out:
   a The type of waste that takes up the most space in our bins.
   b One type of waste that takes up the least space in our bins.

2 Scan Text 1 to answer these questions. Remember: when scanning, identify a key word in the question, then scan the text to find that word.

   a How much of our waste is put into landfill sites?

   b What is produced when waste is incinerated?

   c What does *landfill* mean? Use Text 2 to help you.

Text 2 is part of a glossary from a website that encourages recycling:

Text 2

Kerbside recycling
Also known as **collect schemes**, these are schemes where households put recyclable material in special containers on the roadside outside their homes for collection by the local authority or a waste contractor.

Landfill
Most rubbish collected from homes in the UK is buried in large holes in the ground (often old quarries) called landfill sites.

Leachate
Liquid that drains from a landfill site. It consists of a mixture of rainwater and rotten organic materials.

3 A glossary is like a mini-dictionary: it explains the meaning of difficult words in a particular text or subject.

   a Why do some texts have a glossary?

   b What do you notice about the organisation of the glossary?

   c Where could you look to find more information about landfill sites? Use Text 3 to help you.

Sharpen your skills — Colons and semi-colons

A colon can be used to introduce a list, for example:
The average household bin contains: paper and card, organic matter, metal, glass, etc.

colon   semi-colon

1 Use a colon and a list to complete these two sentences.
- The ingredients for a cheese and pickle sandwich are…
- My favourite things in the whole world are…

A semi-colon is sometimes used to join two clauses in a sentence, taking the place of a conjunction like *and* or *but*. So:

I love listening to loud music but the neighbours hate it
could be written as:
I love listening to loud music ~~but~~; the neighbours hate it

2 Rewrite these sentences using a semi-colon:
   a My sister is really good at cooking and she makes delicious cakes.
   b My dog's breath smells but my brother smells worse.

Text 3 is the index from a science book for students:

Text 3

Index

4 What do you notice about the organisation of the entries in
   the index?

5 How could you use this text to help you find more
   information on landfill?

6 Where do you normally find the index in a book?

Assess your progress

1 In this unit you will learn about writing to argue. Using all the information
   sources available to you, find and write down:
   a a definition of 'writing to argue'.
   b the definitions of three language techniques often used in writing
      to argue. Choose from: **alliteration**, **emotive language**, **repetition**,
      rhetorical questions.

2 a Which information sources did you use?
   b Which ways of finding information can you use confidently?
   c Which ways of finding information do you find more difficult?

2 Aiming at a target audience

You are learning:
- to direct your writing and presentation to appeal to a specific audience.

We also use names in different ways in different situations. For example, we wear different clothes for different occasions – and it is important to get the right clothes for the right occasion. The same is true of the words we use. Some are appropriate to a formal situation, some are more suited to an informal situation.

Activity 1

These three speakers are talking about recycling.

A 'We should not dispose of waste. We should recycle whenever possible.'

B 'Don't just bin your junk. Recycle it!'

C 'Don't throw your rubbish in the dustbin. Try to recycle it.'

1 What situation could each of them be in?
2 Who do you think they are talking to?
3 Which uses the most formal language?
4 Which uses the most informal language?

Activity 2

Many texts are written to appeal to a specific audience: the target audience. This may be people of a particular age group, or with a particular interest. Look at these magazine covers:

1 For each one, write a sentence describing its target audience.

2 Would you expect the language used in these magazines to be more formal or more informal?

Activity 3

Look at these two extracts from websites, explaining what climate change or global warming means.

One says it aims to provide 'a forum for the development of pragmatic policies and solutions to address the most pressing global environmental problem of the twenty-first century.'

The other website says it aims to 'help you explore your environment and learn how to protect it. We've got games, pictures, and stories'.

1   Match each of the extracts above to the correct website.

2   How would you describe the target audiences of these websites?

3   Compare how these extracts appeal to their target audiences. What do you notice about:

- **Presentation** – how the texts look. Try to comment on:
  - the use of colour
  - the use of images
- **Language** – the way the writers have written the texts. Try to comment on:
  - the length of the sentences
  - the kinds of words used
  - whether the language used is formal or informal
  - the use of questions in Text A
  - the links in Text A: what do you think would happen if you clicked on them? Why?

Website A

Climate change: what is it?

Earth has warmed by about 1ºF over the past 100 years. But why? And how? Well, scientists are not exactly sure. The Earth could be getting warmer on its own, but many of the world's leading climate scientists think that things people do are helping to make the Earth warmer.

Website B

Global warming basics

The scientific community has reached a strong consensus regarding the science of global climate change. The world is undoubtedly warming.

This warming is largely the result of emissions of carbon dioxide and other greenhouse gases from human activities including industrial processes, fossil fuel combustion, and changes in land use, such as deforestation.

Sharpen your skills — Active and passive voice

Sometimes we use the passive voice to say what's happened – and to hide who did it. Write three more sentences in the active voice, confessing other terrible things you have done; then put them into the passive voice to hide your guilt. (They don't have to be true confessions!)

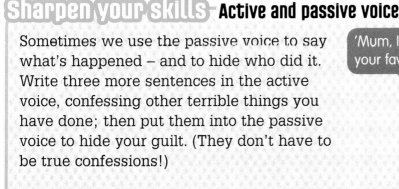

'Mum, I've ripped your favourite skirt!'

active voice

'Mum, your favourite skirt has been ripped!'

passive voice

3 Identifying the main points

You are learning:

- to follow an argument by identifying the key points.

To understand and respond to an argument, you need to be able to identify the key points the writer is making.

Activity 1

Most scientists believe that we are polluting our planet and changing our climate. Some scientists disagree. They think that changes to the Earth's temperature can be explained by more natural causes. The following text supports this argument.

Read the text and answer the questions to learn how to identify the key points the writer is making.

Save the planet, eat a vegan

1 Good news. It seems that your car and your fondness for sunken light bulbs in every alcove are not warming up the planet after all.

2 In fact, according to EarthSave, methane, which pours from a cow's bottom on an industrial scale every few minutes, is 21 times more powerful as a greenhouse gas than carbon dioxide. And as a result, farmed animals are doing more damage to the climate than all the world's transport and power stations put together.

3 EarthSave is encouraging us to stop eating all forms of animal products. No more milk. No more cheese. And if it can be proven that bees fart, then no more honey either. You've got to become a vegan.

4 Now of course if you don't like the taste of meat, then it's perfectly reasonable to become a vegablist. But becoming a vegan? Short of being paraded on the internet while wearing a fluffy pink tutu, I can think of nothing I'd like less.

5 Of course there are certain weeds I like very much. Cauliflower and leeks particularly. But these are an accompaniment to food, useful only for filling up the plate and absorbing the gravy. The idea of eating only a cauliflower, without even so much as a cheese sauce, fills me with dread.

6 So plainly the best thing we can do if we want to save the world and keep on eating meat, is to work out a way that animals can be made to produce less methane.

7 Scientists in Germany are working on a pill that helps, but apparently this has a number of side effects. These are not itemised, but I can only assume that if you trap the gas inside the cow one of the drawbacks is that it might explode. Nasty.

8 At the moment, largely, cows eat grass and silage, and as we've seen, this is melting the ice caps and killing us all. So they need a new foodstuff: something that is rich in iron, calcium and natural goodness.

9 Plainly they can't eat meat so here's an idea to chew on. Why don't we feed them vegetarians?

1. Look at the title of the text. Use it to write one sentence that sums up the writer's point of view.

2. Each paragraph in a text usually contains one key point. The second paragraph in the text contains 54 words. Try to sum up its key point in 15 words or less.

3. Often the key point in a paragraph is made in the first sentence. What is the key point being made in the third paragraph?

4. What is the key point in paragraph four? Did you find it in the first sentence, or did you have to read the whole paragraph to find it?

5. Re-read paragraph five. What is the key point here?

6. Paragraphs six and seven give a possible solution to the problem. What evidence is given in the text to suggest that the writer is unsure that this is an effective solution to the problem?

7. Paragraphs eight and nine give another possible solution. What does it suggest about:
   a. the writer's attitude to the problem?
   b. the writer's attitude to vegetarians?

Activity 2

As well as being able to identify the main points in a written text, you need to be able to identify the main points made in a discussion.

Working in pairs, choose one of the following topics:
- Father Christmas does not exist.
- Children should be encouraged to buy more sweets.
- The weekend should be cut to one day.

One of you will support the argument and the other will argue against it. Write down five points that will help you win the argument; do not show them to your partner.

Discuss your chosen topic with your partner, using your points to try to persuade them that your point of view is the right one. Try to:
- listen carefully to your partner
- respond to their points – don't just read out your own points, one after the other
- ask your partner questions that will defeat their argument.

After the discussion, write down a list of the key points your partner made. Compare your list with theirs. Did you find all their key points?

Sharpen your skills - Prefixes

A prefix is a string of letters that can be added to the front of a word to alter its meaning. Sometimes this creates an opposite: adding *un-* to the front of *important* creates *unimportant*. *Pre-* is a prefix meaning *earlier*, *before* or *in front of*.

1. For each of the words below, write a definition that includes the word *before*.

   prevent **prearrange**
   premature **preview**

2. Now look at these four word endings: *-vent*, *-arrange*, *-mature*, *-view*, and suggest other prefixes that can go in front of them to create new words.

4 Getting your point across

You are learning:

● to identify persuasive language and give a speech effectively.

When a writer or speaker argues their point of view, they do not just use their ideas to persuade us. We are also persuaded by the language they choose.

Activity 1

Below is an extract from a speech made by Charles Kennedy MP, in which he tries to persuade his audience that the Liberal Democrat party cares about environmental issues.

What price our planet?

We know people are concerned about the kind of world our children will inherit, and they are worried about the legacy we are creating for them.

It is not that people don't care about the environment, but people often see the environment as a huge issue affecting the planet, almost too huge, not something they themselves can directly affect.

We need to bring the environmental debate into local communities, and right into people's daily lives.

Not by ignoring the big issues like climate change, but by bringing home to people just how affected they are by the environment on their doorstep.

Being green is about the decisions we take on the things we buy and even how we carry them home.

It is about local planning decisions, taken by local people, in local town halls.

It is about the place we work in – the creation of emissions by the companies we work for, and the products we produce.

And ultimately, it is about our Government being willing to take tough decisions at home and convince other governments across the globe to take those tough decisions too.

Challenging behaviour in the home, challenging the behaviour of our businesses, and challenging the behaviour of governments on the international stage.

Purpose bank

Persuade, Argue, Advise

Inform, Explain, Describe

Analyse, Review, Comment

1　What is the purpose of this speech? Choose one or more of the words in the 'Purpose bank'.

2 Who do you think might be Charles Kennedy's target audience for this speech?

3 a How would you describe the language Charles Kennedy uses in this speech? Is it formal or informal? Standard English or slang?

b How does this choice of language suit his purpose and audience?

4 Using the glossary below, try to identify examples of persuasive language in the speech.

Glossary of rhetorical devices

Alliteration: The repetition of a letter or sound, usually at the start of two or more words in a sentence. Gives a dramatic tone or emphasises a point. *This senseless suffering must stop.*

Direct address: using the pronoun *you* to talk directly to the audience, often to encourage action. *You can make this happen.*

Emotional appeal: an idea intended to create an emotional response, e.g. sympathy. Often refers to children, the elderly, animals. *Imagine how you would feel if this happened to your family.*

Emotive language: a word chosen to create an emotional response in the audience, e.g. sympathy, anger, etc. *Businesses are being forced to make savage cuts.*

First person plural: use of the pronoun *we* to create a feeling of unity between speaker and audience. *None of us can do this alone. We must work together.*

Pattern of three: a list of three words or phrases, sometimes linked by repetition. *This will affect every single one of us: men, women and children.*

Repetition: using a word or phrase more than once to emphasise a point. *We must not give up, we must fight, and fight until we win.*

Rhetorical device: a way of using language to influence an audience.

Rhetorical question: a question that does not expect an answer but leads the audience to the answer which the writer wants. *Should we really be encouraging our children to eat more chips?*

Activity 2

Explore how to deliver a speech.

1 Read the speech aloud. Follow the words closely – don't look up from the text.

2 Now try *delivering* the speech: look at your audience as often as possible and try to say the words as if you mean them. What is the difference between reading a speech aloud and delivering it?

Sharpen your skills · Homophones

Homophones are words that sound the same but have different meanings and spellings.

Write a sentence for each of the following words to show you understand its meaning:

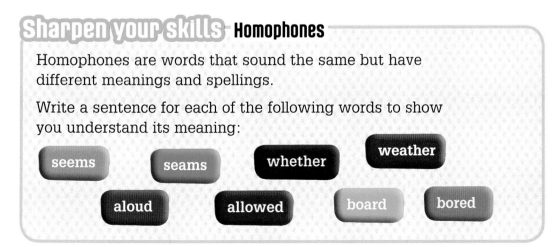

seems   seams   whether   weather

aloud   allowed   board   bored

Activity 3

Using a speech to get your point of view across can be effective, but you must use all the tools you have. The most effective are your voice and your body. How you control them during a speech can win or lose an argument. Look at the control panel on the right.

1   Choose two or three sentences from the speech on page 144. Write a set of instructions on how to deliver them using the control panel, for example:

[**tone:** *concerned*] We [**volume:** *up*] need [**volume:** *down*] to bring the environmental debate into local communities, [**pause**] and right [**tone:** *excited* **Gesture:** *finger point*] into people's daily lives.

2   Practise delivering these sentences to a partner. Can they suggest ways to make your delivery even more effective?

Sharpen your skills – Prepositions

Prepositions are short words that carry a lot of meaning. They explain the relationship between a noun, adjective or pronoun and the rest of the sentence.

1   Try putting each of the prepositions below into the blank space in the sentence 'He ran _____ the road.' How is the meaning changed?

along   up   down   on   past   near

2   Write the sentence starter 'He worked…' three times. Add a different preposition to each one, then complete the sentences. How do the prepositions change the meaning of the word *worked*?

Assess your progress

You have been asked to write a speech arguing that schools should teach subjects that are more relevant to students, such as 'Playing Computer Games', or 'Fashion Tips'.

1 Write up to five sentences that could have come from your speech. Include five of the rhetorical devices listed in the glossary on page 145.

2 Deliver your sentences to a partner as effectively as you can. Use as many of the features as you can from the control panel at the top of this page.

3 Which rhetorical devices did you find difficult to write?

4 Which delivery controls did you find difficult to use?

Assessment task

Speaking and Listening: Listening and responding

Fabspend – the way forward

Listen to the following speech. You can make notes in any way you like during the speech, though remember that you won't be able to write down every word.

Speech from the leader of the local council

1 My fellow councillors, ladies and gentlemen, it is my job this evening to explain to you why the council has decided, after deliberating long and hard, for many months, and listening to the arguments from both sides, **not** to go ahead with either of the original proposals for the area of green space beyond the ring road.

2 It has not been an easy decision and we realise that many of you will be disappointed that the scheme you have supported is not going to go ahead. However, the situation is different now from what it was six months ago, and as the local council responsible for ensuring that you continue to have the high-quality local services you deserve, we have had to make some difficult decisions. None of us feels comfortable with this, but we have reached the point where we believe we have no choice – we have no option but to take this course of action – and we do believe that in the end it will yield the best outcome for the largest number of people.

3 Could I remind you, ladies and gentleman, that you returned our party, The Independent Green Liberation Party, to power in the local elections only two years ago, with a resounding majority of 2000. That was a big vote of confidence – you have to remember how confident you felt then and trust us now to do the best for you in what are very challenging times.

4 The fact is that when we took over as the leading party, the financial situation in this area was not good. Income in the form of council tax has not been covering our outgoings – we are now under pressure to tighten our belts, draw in our horns and look for ways

to cut our cloth according to our means. In short, ladies and gentlemen, we are operating this year with a budget deficit of £1,000,000, a situation which cannot be allowed to continue.

5   It was fortuitous, then, if not something of a miracle, when the supermarket chain Fabspend came forward with an offer we couldn't refuse. They have been looking to expand in our area. Yes, I know they already have one store on the west of the town, but they are now looking to build up a customer base on the east side as well. They too have been looking at the green space site – and they see it as an ideal location for their new store. Their market research has revealed that 82 per cent of local residents would welcome a Fabspend store in that location and that it will really be meeting a market need in the area.

6   Fabspend have also offered to provide a play area for young children in their in-store café and, to show their commitment to the environment, to sponsor a tree sapling in the town centre. There is no doubt that Fabspend are very sensitive to the issues around this particular site and mindful of their duty to respect local customs and views. We should remember too, that when the new Fabspend store opens, not only will the retail options of local people be expanded, but there will be employment opportunities too.

7   We will, of course, be taking questions from the floor, but before I open up the discussion, I would like to ask the Regional Area Manager for Fabspend to say a few words to you.

Your task

You can ask the leader of the council to explain any words or phrases that you did not understand; then you should complete the activities below.

1 Give one word, phrase or number in answer to the following questions:
   a How long has the Green Independent Liberation party been in power?
   b How big was their majority?
   c How big is the budget deficit
   d Who is going to build on the green space?
   e Name one thing that this company is going to do for the local community.

2 In one sentence, sum up the main point of the speech.

3 Give one way the leader of the council tries to show that the council has found it difficult to come to this decision.

4 Explain one way the leader of the council tries to persuade the audience to trust him.

5 Write down three questions you would like to ask the leader of the council.

6 Write down three questions you would like to ask the Regional Area Manager for Fabspend.

7 Does this speech help persuade you that the council has made the right decision? Give reasons for your answer.

5 Note-making

You are learning:

- to make notes to summarise information and help your understanding.

You will often need to make notes during your time at school and at work. It is a way of making a lot of information smaller and clearer. It also helps you pick out and understand the key points of a text you are reading.

Activity 1

1 Read this extract from a website called 'Greener living: a quick guide to what you can do'. Then read Methods A to C, which show you three different ways of making notes.

2 Decide which method provides notes about which of the paragraphs from the website.

---

http://www.direct.gov.uk

Save energy and water at home

1 Burning fossil fuels to heat our homes or produce electricity releases carbon emissions, which cause climate change. The energy you use at home is likely to be your biggest contribution to climate change. 80 per cent of it goes on heating and hot water, so this is a good place to look for savings.

2 **Turn down your thermostat**

Turning your thermostat down by one degree could reduce carbon emissions and cut your fuel bills by up to 10 per cent.

3 **Look for the labels**

When buying products that use energy – anything from light bulbs to fridge-freezers – look for the Energy Saving Recommended label or European energy label rating of A or higher. The European energy label also tells you how much water appliances use, so you can choose a more efficient model.

4 **Improve your insulation**

More than half the heat lost in your home escapes through the walls and roof. Cavity wall insulation costs about £260, can take a couple of hours to install, and could save you £160 a year on fuel bills.

Method A
You can use key words, symbols and abbreviations to make notes. They look like this:

Point: Fossil fuel > heat/electricity = carbon emissions = climate change.
Evidence: 80% energy used in home for heating/hot water.

Method B

Or you can use bullet points or a table. They look like this:

- **Point:** Turn down your thermostat
- **Evidence:** It reduces carbon emissions and cuts fuel bills by 10%

Point	Evidence
Turn down your thermostat	It reduces carbon emissions and cuts fuel bills by 10%

The key points are organised in a list. You can add columns to the table to add information or develop your ideas.

Method C

Or you can use a diagram like this:

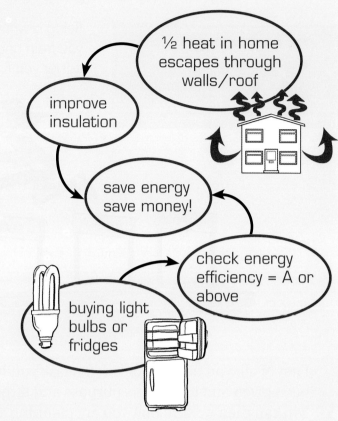

The key points are linked to a central idea and to one another. You can use words and pictures to organise the information. This is more flexible than a list – you can see how all the ideas are connected.

Assess your progress

1 Use the three different methods to make notes on each of the three paragraphs in this extract from the same website.

2 Which method of note-making do you:
- find easiest?
- think is most effective?

http://www.direct.gov.uk

→Recycle more

Nearly two-thirds of all household rubbish can be recycled. Most councils run doorstep recycling collections for paper, glass and plastics, often more. But local civic amenity sites often accept many other things – from wood and shoes, to textiles and TVs.

→Get composting

Composting food waste reduces climate-change effects. Many local councils offer subsidised compost bins or a home collection for kitchen and garden waste.

→Re-use and repair

Avoiding waste in the first place, by re-using and repairing items, is the most efficient way to reduce waste. For example, buy items that can be re-used rather than disposables, and pass things on when you've finished with them.

6 Organising ideas

You are learning:
- to plan and sequence your ideas for extended writing.

Being a writer is like being an athlete. The more you train and practise, the better you get – and the easier you find it.

Activity 1

First of all, you need to look at the task you have been given and identify its purpose and target audience. You can then be sure that you are planning a piece of writing that will do what it needs to do – before you write it.

Look at these two tasks.

A   You represent your year group on the school council. Write a speech in which you argue that the school should do more to make itself environmentally friendly.

B   Write an article for your school newsletter, arguing that students are already environmentally aware – it's their parents who need to be greener.

1   Identify the purpose and the audience for the task. You can use the 'Purpose bank' on page 144 to help you. Record your answers in a table like this:

Task	Purpose	Audience
A	Argue	School council
B		

2   For each of these tasks write a sentence that is inappropriate either for the purpose or the intended audience.

3   Think of a new writing task that asks students to argue a case. Make sure your task tells the writer the purpose and audience they are writing for. Swap tasks with a partner. Can they identify the purpose and audience?

Activity 2

Once you have identified your purpose and audience, you need to plan the ideas you will use in your writing. Imagine arguing Task A (that your school should become more environmentally friendly).

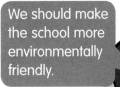

Think of points that will get your opinion across to the reader and use evidence to prove them. If you were planning Task A, you might have read over this unit so far and come up with these three points and three pieces of evidence:

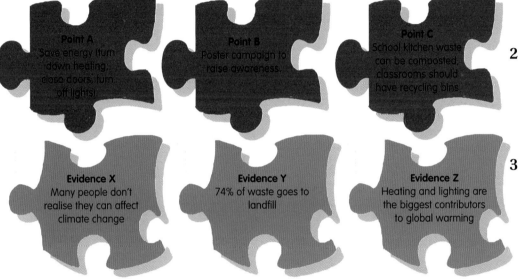

Point A
Save energy (turn down heating, close doors, turn off lights).

Point B
Poster campaign to raise awareness.

Point C
School kitchen waste can be composted, classrooms should have recycling bins.

Evidence X
Many people don't realise they can affect climate change

Evidence Y
74% of waste goes to landfill

Evidence Z
Heating and lighting are the biggest contributors to global warming

1 Which evidence proves which point? Match the points to the evidence.

2 Decide the best order in which to put these points. Write two or three sentences explaining your decision.

3 Re-read Task B and plan the three points and three pieces of evidence you would use. Then sequence your points into the best order.

Sharpen your skills Paragraphs

Paragraphs help readers to understand texts. They divide the story or information into chunks that make their meaning clearer. There are no rules about the length of a paragraph, but there are four reasons to start a new paragraph:
- a change of subject
- a change of time
- a change of place
- a new speaker.

1 Which of the sentences below might you find at the start of a paragraph? Why?
- A hundred years later, in the twentieth century, we began to realise the damage we were doing to our environment.
- It was the first time that scientists understood how this could have happened.
- However, it happened very quickly.
- Another way in which we can prevent global warming is by recycling.
- In America, people were becoming more aware of climate change.
- It was much more difficult than they had imagined.
- 'We can all help,' he replied.

2 You have been asked to write four paragraphs describing your day so far. Write the opening sentence of each paragraph; try to use a different reason for starting each new paragraph.

7 Developing your argument

You are learning:

- to develop your writing to argue by including connectives, a counter-argument and rhetorical devices.

Putting forward a successful argument needs more than just good points. You need to organise and express your argument very carefully.

Activity 1

One successful way to win an argument is to guess what your opponent is going to argue – and be ready to tell them why they are wrong.

1 It's bedtime. Write down three points a parent or carer might make to argue that you should go to bed.

2 For each of those three points, make a counter-argument, arguing that you should stay up for another half hour.

3 Look at the plan you made for writing to argue on page 153, Activity 2, question 3.
   a What point might someone opposing your argument make?
   b What counter-argument could you make to show that they are wrong?

Activity 2

You have now planned four paragraphs of your article arguing for parents to be more environmentally aware. Three of them will support your argument using evidence; the other one will give a counter-argument and then explain why you think it is wrong.

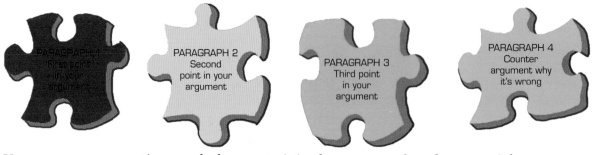

PARAGRAPH 1 First point in your argument

PARAGRAPH 2 Second point in your argument

PARAGRAPH 3 Third point in your argument

PARAGRAPH 4 Counter argument why it's wrong

You can use connectives and phrases to join the paragraphs of your article together. Which of the connectives could go at the start of each paragraph?

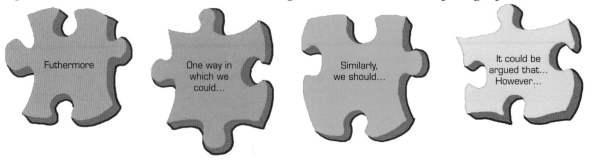

Futhermore

One way in which we could…

Similarly, we should…

It could be argued that… However…

Activity 3

Here are some sentences from one student's argument that schools should be more environmentally friendly (Task A). Rewrite them to make them more persuasive. Try to include as many rhetorical devices as you can (look at the glossary of rhetorical devices on page 145 to help you).

- Throwing all our rubbish into landfill sites is not very good.
- Having the school's heating up too high is bad.
- Also, people should turn off lights when they don't need them.
- The school is wasting energy and damaging the planet.
- Being environmentally friendly is good.

Sharpen your skills — First and third person

Some stories are written in the first person: one of the characters tells the story using the word *I*. Some stories are written in the third person: the narrator uses the words *he*, *she*, *it* and *they* to describe the events of the story.

Writing to argue may use the first person or the third person. Compare these sentences:

- I think that they must do more to help the environment.
- They must do more to help the environment.

1 Which sentence is written in the first person?

2 Which sentence is written in the third person?

3 Which sentence shows that the writer or speaker really means what they say?

4 Which sentence is more powerful and likely to make the reader or listener change their opinion?

5 Which sentence sounds more like a fact than an opinion?

6 Try writing a sentence in the first person and then rewriting it in the third person. Which do you prefer? Why?

Assess your progress

You have been learning how to plan a piece of writing to argue. Now write a set of instructions on how to do this. Remember to include all the different stages you have learnt about. You can look back over pages 147–55 to help you.

8 Draft, revise and proofread

You are learning:
● to turn your plan into a successful piece of writing to argue.

Once you have done the hard work of planning your writing, you need to make the most of it by drafting, then improving, then checking it.

Activity 1

Look back at the work you have done planning your article for Task B on page 152. Now you have planned your points and evidence, you can begin writing. You will need to write six paragraphs:

1. Introduction   2. First point   3. Second point   4. Third point

5. Counter-argument   6. Conclusion

Write a two-sentence introduction to your article, arguing that parents need to be more environmentally friendly. Your introduction needs to explain two things:
● how things are at the moment.
● why you think things should change.

You could begin:
At the moment... The problem is...

Activity 2

When you write your second, third and fourth paragraphs, you should use the points and evidence you have planned. You will need to add an explanation to your point and evidence. The explanation tells your audience how the point and evidence prove your argument.

Write a Point–Evidence–Explain paragraph using the point and evidence below.
● Parents can walk to the shops instead of driving their cars.
● Global warming is largely the result of carbon dioxide emissions.

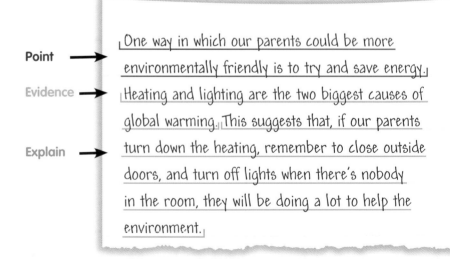

Point → One way in which our parents could be more environmentally friendly is to try and save energy. Evidence → Heating and lighting are the two biggest causes of global warming. This suggests that, if our parents Explain → turn down the heating, remember to close outside doors, and turn off lights when there's nobody in the room, they will be doing a lot to help the environment.

Activity 3

Finally, you need to write your conclusion. This sums up your opinion and tells your audience what you want them to think and do. A good way to do this is to write a few sentences saying what will happen in the future if:

- what you are suggesting doesn't happen. This will be bad.
- what you are suggesting does happen. This will be good.

Write a two-sentence conclusion to your article. You could begin:

If we do not change...

However, if we make the changes I am suggesting...

Activity 4

Now that you have written your first draft, it's time to read it over and improve it. The first thing to do is to check your sentences. You should try to use a range of sentences: long and short, simple, compound and complex (see the 'Sharpen your skills' box on page 158).

1. Rewrite the paragraph on the right, improving the way sentences are used.

> Another way in which we could improve our school is to make students more aware of the problems of global warming and how we need to do more to stop it because a lot of people don't realise that we can do things to help the environment and we could do that by getting Year 7 students to design posters and we could put them up around the school and maybe have assemblies about it. To get more people interested.

2. You need to check your spelling and punctuation. Writers often make mistakes – but careful checking and correcting are things that make the difference between a piece of writing and a **good** piece of writing. See how many mistakes you can find in the paragraph on the right.

    a. How many mistakes did you find on each line?
    b. What are the mistakes?

> i think their is one other thing we should do every year seven class should be given a flour bed to look after They can grow vegtubles or flowers. growing things make people more aware of the inviroment and nature. it would help us see that we can chang the world and make it a better place to be.

3. If you have done your writing on a computer, then you don't need to check the spelling – the spellchecker has done that for you, right?

    Wrong! A spellchecker will find no spelling mistakes in this sentence…

    Yew knead two cheque watt ewe right sew ewe our shore their our know missed aches.

    …but it's completely wrong. Why?

Sharpen your skills - Simple, compound and complex sentences

1 Simple sentences contain only one verb. The dog chased the cat.

   Write four simple sentences. Remember to include capital letters and full stops. Underline the verb in each of your sentences.

2 Compound sentences contain two verbs. You can create them by joining two simple sentences using *and* or *but*.

   The dog chased the cat. He did not catch it. becomes The dog chased the cat but he did not catch it.

   Try to join your simple sentences into two compound sentences using *and* or *but*.

3 Complex sentences contain two verbs. They also use connectives to join them, such as *because*, *although*, *whenever* or *if* – but they have different rules:

   • One half of a complex sentence does not make sense on its own.
   • You can swap the two halves round to change the emphasis without changing the meaning.

   The dog chased the cat. They were enemies. becomes The dog chased the cat because they were enemies. which means the same as Because they were enemies, the dog chased the cat.

Try to join your simple sentences into two complex sentences using *because*, *although*, *whenever* or *if*. Remember to include capital letters and full stops. Use the two rules of complex sentences to test whether they really are complex sentences.

Assess your progress

Below is a list of all the stages of writing you have learnt about in this unit.
For each one, write two or three sentences explaining what writers should remember to do to make their planning, drafting, revising and proofreading successful.

Remember:

1. Make notes	2. Plan your paragraphs	3. Write your first draft	4. Improve your writing	5. Check your writing
• •	• • •	• • •	• • •	• •

Assessment task
Writing: Composition and conventions

Recreation ground – yes or no?

There is a plan to build a new recreation ground with a paddling pool, skateboard ramp and rose garden on a green space near you. This plan has divided the local community.

Some people think it is a good idea.

Other people think the green space should be kept as a natural habitat for wild plants and animals.

Your task

Write a leaflet persuading local people to join the campaign **either** for the new recreation ground **or** against it. You should decide:

- whether your leaflet will be **for** the new recreation ground or **against** it
- who you are aiming your leaflet at
- what arguments you are going to use to persuade your readers to support the campaign.

You do not need to produce pictures, but you could indicate where photographs or plans might go.

You will be assessed on:

- your awareness of purpose and audience
- the organisation and presentation of the whole of your leaflet
- your use of persuasive language.

Heinemann is an imprint of Pearson Education Limited, a company incorporated in England and Wales, having its registered office at Edinburgh Gate, Harlow, Essex, CM20 2JE. Registered company number: 872828

www.heinemann.co.uk

Heinemann is the registered trademark of Pearson Education Limited

Text © Pearson Education Limited 2008

First published 2008

13

10 9

British Library Cataloguing in Publication Data is available from the British Library on request.

ISBN 978 0 435579 77 7

Designed and produced by Kamae Design, Oxford
Original illustrations © Harcourt Education Limited 2008
Illustrated by Kathryn Baker, Humberto Blanco, Paco Cavero, Serena Curmi, Marjorie Dumortier, Tony Forbes, Mike Lacey, Laura Martinez, Paul McCaffrey, Andrew Quelch, Jo Taylor
Cover design by Pete Stratton
Picture research by Caitlin Swain
Cover illustration by Andrew Painter
Printed in China (GCC/09)

Acknowledgements

The author and publisher would like to thank the following individuals and organisations for permission to reproduce photographs:

Rex Features/ Justin Williams p11; Rex Features/ Richard Austin pp5, 14 (top left); PA Photos pp5 (middle right), 18, 19, 21; Corbis/ Najlah Feanny pp5 (bottom), 24; Corbis/ Jeff Vanuga p14; Rex Features p20; Bradley Kanaris / Getty Images pp22, 23; Rex Features/ Animal Planet/Everett p26; Rex Features/ Peter Barnes pp28, 29, 30; Corbis/ John Lund pp31, 32; Getty Images/ Photonica p37; Digital Stock p37; RSPCA Photolibrary pp40,52 (left and right), 53; Rex Features/ Julian Simmonds p42; Alamy Images p46; Getty Images/ Photodisc pp50, 51, 122 (top right); Corbis/ Daniel J. Cox p54; Istockphoto.com pp55, 56; Lebrecht Music and Arts Photo Library / Alamy p59; Photos 12 / Alamy p59; Rex Features/ Huw John p60; Popperfoto/Alamy p66; The Art Archive/ Private Collection / Marc Charmet p74; Getty Images/ Hulton Archive pp76, 77; creacart / Istockphoto p84 (bottom circle); Robert Frith / Istockphoto p84 (middle circle); Rex Features/ Stephen Lock p84 (top circle); National Portrait Gallery, London p84 (bottom right); Corbis/ Moodboard p85; Digital Vision pp97, 135 (middle), 138, 139; Photofusion/ Paul Baldesare p98; Alamy Images/ Gari Wyn Williams p99, 104; Getty Images/ Time & Life Pictures p107 (top left); Photolibrary.com/ p107 (top right); Photofusion/ Paul Doyle p107 (middle left); Alamy Images/ Ulrich Doering p107 (middle right); Alamy Images/ Nicholas Pitt p107 (bottom left); Rex Features/ Sipa Press p107 (bottom right); Pearson Education Ltd / Tudor Photography p120; Jose Manueal / Dreamstime p122 (top left); Corbis/ Dennis Galante p122 (middle); Getty Images/PhotoDisc p122 (bottom right); Corbis/ Randy Faris p122 (bottom middle); Getty Images/Brand X Pictures p122 (bottom left); Photos.com p125 (top left); Danish Khan / Istockphoto p125 (top right); Michael Kempter / Istockphoto p125 (bottom left); Getty Images/ Robert Harding World Imagery p125 (bottom right); Robert Byran / Istockphoto p135 (top); NASA p135 (bottom); Corbis pp142, 143; Getty Images/ Bruno Vincent p144.

Every effort has been made to contact copyright holders of material reproduced in this book. Any omissions will be rectified in subsequent printings if notice is given to the publishers.

Cover of Diana: Her True Story – in Her Own Words by Andrew Morton, published by Michael O'Mara Books Limited. Reproduced by permission of the publisher. Photograph © Patrick Demarchelier; Cover of Cilla Black: What's it all about? Published by Ebury Press 2003. Reprinted with permission of The Random House Group Limited; Cover of The Gospel According to Chris Moyles by Chris Moyles, published by Ebury Press. Reprinted with permission of The Random House Group Limited; Cover of London the Biography by Peter Ackroyd, published by Vintage. Reprinted with permission of The Random House Group Ltd; Cover of Zig Zag by Nicholas Booth, published by Piatkus. Reprinted with permission of Piatkus Books; Cover and blurb from Welcome to my World by Coleen McCoughlin, published by HarperCollins Publishers. Reprinted with permission of HarperCollins Publishers Ltd; Cover and blurb from Telling Tales by Alan Bennett, published by BBC Books. Reprinted with permission of The Random House Group Ltd; Use of an extract from www.benjaminzephaniah.com Copyright © Benjamin Zephaniah. Reprinted with the kind permission of the author; Photograph of Benjamin Zephaniah © Benjamin Zephaniah. Reprinted with the kind permission of the author; Extract from Dare to Dream! 25 Extraordinary Lives by Sandra McLeod Humphrey (Amherst, NY: Prometheus Books, 2005) pp 17–18. Copyright © 2005 by Sandra McLeod Humphrey. Reprinted with permission of the publisher; Extract from 'Leader of the Pack' by Brian Mciver, 11 May 2007, Daily Record. Reprinted with permission of Mirrorpix, Trinity Mirror Print; Extract from Communication from www.autism.org.uk/siblinginfo. Reprinted with permission; Use of an illustration, illustrating the autistic communications text. Copyright © Warren Roome. Reprinted with permission of the illustrator; Ade Adepitan, speech by Charlie Bethel, Monday 17th July. Copyright © Charlie Bethel. Reprinted with permission of the author; Article from CBBC Website about Ade Adepitan. Copyright © CBBC. www.bbc.co.uk/cbbc/sports/sportstars/adepitan.shtml. Reprinted with permission of the BBC; Cover of The Curious Incident of the Dog in the Night-Time by Mark Haddon, published by Vintage. Reprinted with permission of The Random House Group Limited; Extract from 'B is for Bestseller' by Mark Haddon, The Observer, 11 April 2004. Copyright © Mark Haddon 2004. Reprinted with permission of Aitken Alexander Associates Limited; 'Daredevil Irwin dies doing what he loved' September 4th 2006. Copyright © AAP. Reprinted with permission; 'Steve wasn't going to die in bed' by Virginia Wheeler, The Sun, September 5th 2006. Reprinted with permission; 'Interview with Crocodile Hunter Steve Irwin – Part 1: Method to His Madness?' by Sarah Simpson, April 18, 2001 Scientific American website. Reprinted with permission; 'That sort of self delusion is what it takes to be a real aussie larkin' by Germain Greer, originally published in The Guardian, 5th September, 2006. Copyright © Germain Greer. Reprinted with permission of Aitken Alexander Associates Ltd; Front page from The Times, 24th July, 2007. © Times Newspapers. Reprinted with permission; Photograph from the front page of The Times, 24th July, 2007, taken by Dan Kitwood, South West News Services. Reprinted with permission; Front page of the Daily Mirror, 11th January, 2007. Reprinted with permission; 'Are we really becoming more cruel to our pets?' by Trevor Grove, Daily Mail, 27th July 2006. Reprinted with permission of Solo Syndication; Tiny extract from 'Fowl Play, ref' from Daily Mirror, 12th May 2007. Reprinted with permission; Tiny extract from 'Spiders in boy's ear' from Daily Mirror, 8th May, 2007. Reprinted with permission; Tiny extract from 'Mobiles are killing off bees' from Daily Mirror, 16th April 2007. Reprinted with permission; Small extract from 'Case Cat's Plane Adventure' from The Daily Mirror, 3rd May, 2007. Reprinted with permission; 'Boy gets toilet seat stuck on his head' © Reuters. License REU-2006-MES www.reuters.com. Reprinted with permission; Article 'Welcome to Modbury. Just don't ask for a plastic bag' by John Vidal, The Guardian, 28 April 2007. © Guardian News & Media Ltd, 2007. Reprinted with permission; Extract from 'Town axes plastic bags' by Richard Smith, Daily Mail. Reprinted with permission; Extracts from 'Labradors too fat to go for a walk' Daily Mail, 25th April, 2007. Reprinted with permission of Solo Syndication; Article 'Whale stranded in Thames' by Mark Oliver, The Guardian, 20 January 2006. © Guardian News & Media Ltd 2006. Reprinted with permission; Article slightly abridged from 'Classroom thugs told: Disrupt school and win an iPod!' Daily Mail, 26th June, 2007. Reprinted with permission of Solo Syndication; 'On trial for her life, the sausage dog who nipped a neighbour' by Paul Sims, Daily Mail, 26th June, 2007. Reprinted with permission of Solo Syndication; 'Take a last look' by Terry Nutkins, The Guardian 8th November, 2006. Reprinted with kind permission; Extract from Night of the Stick Insects by Alan Durrant published by Orion Children's Books. Reprinted with permission of Orion Children's Books; Extract from Golem's Eye by Jonathan Stroud, published by Doubleday. Reprinted with permission of The Random House Group Ltd; Extracts from Raven's Gate by Anthony Horowitz, published by Walker Books Ltd. Text © 2005 Anthony Horowitz. Reproduced by permission of Walker Books Ltd, London SE11 5HJ; Short extracts from Coraline by Neil Gaiman, published by Bloomsbury Publishing. Reprinted with permission of Bloomsbury Publishing and Dorie Simmonds; 'Be a Butterfly' by Grace Nichols from The Fat Black Woman's Poems published by Virago 1984. Copyright © Grace Nichols 1984. Reproduced by permission of Curtis Brown Group Ltd; Extract from Refugee Boy by Benjamin Zephaniah, published by Bloomsbury. Reprinted with permission of Bloomsbury Plc; Extract from The Return to Beirut by Andree Chedid, published by Serpents Tail. Reprinted with permission of Profile Books; 'Hoodies Banned by Bluewater' May 12 2005, from www.raisingkids.co.uk. Reprinted with permission; 'Call to ban mobile phones in classrooms' June 27th, 2007 Copyright © Press Association. Reprinted with permission; Front cover in its entirety of Everything Bad is Good for You by Steven Johnson (Allen Lane Penguin Press 2005) Copyright © Steven Johnson 2005. Reprinted with permission of Penguin Books; Mock up of homepage from www.teddyfone.com Reprinted with permission; Hello. My name is Bob... by Bob Ivry, first published in The Washington Post's Book World, 2005. Reprinted with kind permission of the author; Extract from The Forest of the Pygmies by Isabelle Allende, published by HarperCollins Publishers. Reprinted with permission of HarperCollins Publishers Ltd; 'Luv Song', 'For Sale', 'No Problem' and 'Pets control' from Talking Turkeys by Benjamin Zephaniah (Viking, 1994) Copyright © Benjamin Zephaniah 1994. Reprinted with permission of Penguin Books; 'The British', 'Urdu Poets', 'The Tourists are coming' and 'The Vegans' from Wicked World by Benjamin Zephaniah. (Puffin 2000) Text Copyright © Benjamin Zephaniah, 2000. Reprinted with permission of Penguin Books; Audio rights in poems by Benjamin Zephaniah Copyright © Benjamin Zephaniah. Readings used with kind permission of Benjamin Zephaniah; 'I luv me mudder' by Benjamin Zephaniah, rewritten for The Bloomsbury Book of Love Poems edited by Benjamin Zephaniah, 1999 © 1999 Benjamin Zephaniah. Reprinted with kind permission of the author; Use of photograph of Benjamin Zephaniah © Benjamin Zephaniah. Reprinted with kind permission of the author; 'Mother to Son' by Langston Hughes, from Collected Poems of Langston Hughes published by Alfred A. Knopf Inc. Reprinted with permission of David Higham Associates Limited; Use of www.recyclenow.com/start recycling/index.html. Reprinted with permission of The Guides Network; Use of graphic of bin adapted from leaflet 'What's in your bin?' and facts from www.wasteconnect.co.uk. Copyright © e4environment. Reprinted with kind permission of e4environment Ltd; Crown Copyright materials reproduced with permission of the controller of the HMSO; Extract – Index page from Where Does Rubbish Go? Reproduced by permission of Usborne Publishing, 83–85 Saffron Hill, London EC1N 8RT UK www.usborne.com. Copyright © Usborne Publishing Ltd; Use of a cover from People's Friend. Reprinted with permission of D. C. Thomson & Co Ltd; Use of cover from Shout magazine. Reprinted with permission of D. C. Thomson & Co Ltd; Use of September 2007 Cover of Practical Parenting Magazine Copyright © Practical Parenting/IPC+ Syndication. Reprinted with permission; Extract re: climate change from www.epa.gov Reprinted with permission; 'Global warming basics' from www.pewclimate.org reprinted with permission; Article adapted 'Save the planet, eat a vegan' by Jeremy Clarkson, The Sunday Times, 3 June, 2007. Reprinted with permission of NI Syndication; Use of an extract from speech What Price our Planet? by Charles Kennedy. Copyright © Charles Kennedy. Reprinted with the kind permission of Charles Kennedy.

Text

Building skills in English Book 1: Levels 3–5

Text – Building skills in English 11-14 provides exciting, comprehensive coverage of the National Curriculum's Programme of Study and the Renewed English Framework. It builds students' Functional Skills and uses APP-style assessments to help progress.

Objectives tell students what they will learn about and learn to do.

The Student Book and additional activities are all available on LiveText.

Texts are drawn from a range of National Curriculum recommended authors, each with their biography.

'Assess your progress' features help check progression and inform students what they need to do to improve, level by level.

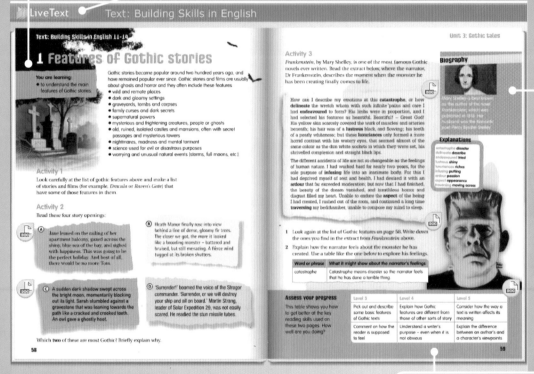

- 'Sharpen your skills' activities in the book and on the LiveText CD ROM help build students' technical accuracy.

- Two APP-style Assessment Tasks per unit aid in student assessment and planning of next steps.

Text: Building Skills in English 11-14

www.heinemann.c
01865 88808

ISBN 978-0-435579-
9 780435 5797

KU-808-386